AN EXPOSITION

OF THE

AFRICAN SLAVE TRADE,

FROM THE YEAR 1840, TO 1850, INCLUSIVE.

PREPARED FROM OFFICIAL DOCUMENTS,

AND

PUBLISHED BY DIRECTION OF THE REPRESENTATIVES OF THE RELIGIOUS SOCIETY OF FRIENDS,

IN

PENNSYLVANIA, NEW JERSEY, AND DELAWARE.

PHILADELPHIA:

FOR SALE AT FRIENDS' BOOK STORE, NO. 84 MULBERRY STREET.
J. RAKESTRAW, PRINTER.

1851.

PREFACE.

In the preparation of the following pages, we have relied for authority chiefly on the "Slave Trade Papers," presented to both Houses of Parliament in Great Britain, and by them ordered to be published.

The papers of each year are divided into four classes, A, B, C and D, each constituting a volume, to which reference is made in noting our extracts. Some extracts have likewise been taken from the printed evidence, given before the Committees of Parliament, appointed on the Slave Trade question.

Most of the important testimony, relating to the participation of American citizens in the traffic, is derived from official communications of foreign ministers and officers of the United States, many of them having been published by direction of the Senate.

AN EXPOSITION

OF THE

AFRICAN SLAVE TRADE.

It cannot be denied, that the African Slave trade had its origin from, and owes its continuance to, the cupidity of unprincipled men. Its first steps are indelibly marked with violence and bloodshed, and every subsequent stage is inseparably connected with misery and suffering—landing both the victims and their oppressors in degradation and wretchedness. So generally is the knowledge of these facts spread throughout the world, that there are none among the nations professing Christianity, and but few of those styled barbarous, who have not either altogether prohibited their citizens from engaging in the traffic, or enacted laws to restrain them in its prosecution, and to regulate the mode in which it may be carried on, so as in some measure to diminish its horrors. Few governments have taken more decided ground in this respect, or placed upon their statute book laws more stringent, or more unequivocal against any of its citizens engaging, or being in any way interested, in the African Slave trade, than have these United States.

So early as 1794, an Act was passed, prohibiting under a severe penalty, any citizen or other person residing within the United States, from building or equipping any vessel for the purpose of carrying on the traffic in slaves to any foreign country, or for the purpose of transporting slaves from one foreign country to another; and in 1798, 1800, and 1803, respectively, laws were enacted, defining this offence in its several forms, and more particularly, seeking to guard, by penalties of fine, forfeiture and imprisonment, against any of those residing within the jurisdiction of the United States, being implicated in, or accessory to its commission.

In 1807, a law was enacted, totally prohibiting the importation into any part of the United States, from any foreign country, of any negro, mulatto, or person of colour, for the purpose of holding or selling such person as a slave; and also prohibiting any citizen, or other person residing within the country from building, equipping, or preparing within its jurisdiction, any vessel to be employed in the importation of slaves into the United States; and forbidding all from engaging in such importation. Severe penalties were attached to the infraction of these laws; and in 1818, the same penalties were extended to the act of preparing vessels for the transportation of slaves to any place whatever.

These various Acts failing to effect all that was desired, a law was passed in 1820, declaring that any citizen of the United States, being of the crew or ship's company of any foreign vessel engaged in the Slave trade; or any person whatever, being of the crew of a vessel owned wholly or in part by, or navigated for or on behalf of, any citizen of the United States, who shall land on any foreign shore, and seize any negro or mulatto, not held to service by the laws of any state or territory of the United States; or who shall decoy, or forcibly bring on board such vessel, any such negro or mulatto, with intent of holding such negro or mulatto as a slave; every such person so offending, shall be adjudged a pirate, and on conviction thereof shall suffer death. This law also provides, that if any citizen of the United States, being of the crew or ship's company of any foreign vessel engaged in the slave trade, or any person whatever, being of the ship's company of any vessel, owned wholly or in part by, or navigated on behalf of, any citizen of the United States, shall forcibly confine or detain, or shall abet in forcibly confining or detaining, on board any such vessel, any negro or mulatto, not held to service or labour by the laws of either of the states or territories of the United States, with intent to make such negro or mulatto a slave; or shall on board any such vessel, offer or attempt to sell as a slave, any negro or mulatto not held to service as aforesaid; or shall on the high seas, or any where on tide water, transfer or deliver over to any other ship or vessel, any negro or mulatto, not held to service as aforesaid, with intent to make such negro or mulatto a slave; or shall land or deliver on shore, from on board such ship or vessel, any such negro or mulatto, with intent to make sale of, or having previously sold such negro or mulatto as a slave, such citizen or person shall be adjudged a pirate, and on conviction thereof shall suffer death.

In the year 1807, after long and persevering exertions on the part of Clarkson, Wilberforce and many others, an Act was passed by the British Parliament, prohibiting the subjects of that government from any participation in the African Slave trade. Since that period, other laws have been passed more effectually to secure the design of that act, and by which those engaging in that trade were declared guilty of felony; and in 1824, that traffic was by the statutes of that country, as it is by the United States, declared to be piracy.

Since 1807, the year in which she first prohibited her own subjects from engaging in the slave trade, Great Britain has repeatedly urged the subject upon the attention of the different powers, both in Europe and America, with whom treaties have been made by her, and solicited them to co-operate with her in its complete extinction.

In 1813, Sweden bound herself by treaty, not to permit her subjects to engage in the trade; and Denmark, whose king so early as 1792, had issued a decree prohibiting his subjects from purchasing, selling or transporting slaves, acquiesced in the justice of the measure, and prohibited the trade absolutely by her municipal laws.

France, Austria, Russia and Prussia, in reply to the suggestions of the British ministers, expressed their abhorrence of the traffic, and their determination to co-operate in its abolition. In the treaties of Paris, Kiël and Ghent, in 1814, it was stipulated that the odious traffic in slaves from Africa should be abolished, which stipulation was confirmed by the Congress of the Allied Powers at Vienna in 1815, and they declared their wish "to put an end to a scourge which desolates Africa, degrades Europe, and afflicts humanity;" and in the treaty of peace concluded at Paris in that year, an additional article was annexed, by which the contracting parties pledged themselves to renewed exertions for the total extinction of a commerce, so repugnant to every principle of justice and humanity.

The King of France, in 1815, issued an edict, prohibiting the trade to his subjects, from that time and forever.

The accession of Portugal and Spain to the principle of the abolition of the trade, was obtained by the treaties between Great Britain and those Powers respectively, in 1815, and 1817. Spain, in the latter year, restricted her subjects engaged in the trade, from going north of the line to prosecute it. In 1820, this prohibition was extended to all places south of the equator. And in 1845, she enacted a stringent penal law, for the purpose of suppressing the trade.

In 1815, Portugal confined this trade carried on by her subjects, to the south of the line. In 1836, she issued a decree, declaring the final and entire abolition of the Portuguese slave trade. And in 1842, she issued a decree, declaring the traffic within all her dominions to be piracy, and subjecting those found engaged in it to severe penalties.

The King of the Netherlands, in 1814, entirely interdicted the trade to his subjects; and in 1818, entered into a treaty with Great Britain for its total suppression.

In 1813, Sweden bound herself by treaty, not to permit her subjects to engage in the trade; and in 1824, concluded another treaty for its abolition. Sardinia, Tuscany, Naples, and the Hanse Towns, respectively, between the years 1834 and 1838, acceded to the terms of the convention agreed on between Great Britain and France, in 1831 and 1833, for the abolition of the slave trade.

By a convention concluded between Great Britain and Brazil in 1826, it was stipulated that three years after the exchange of the ratifications, it should not be lawful for the subjects of the Emperor of Brazil to be concerned in carrying on the African slave trade, and that the carrying on of such trade by any subject of Brazil, should be deemed and treated as piracy.

In 1831, the Emperor, issued a decree, by which he declared, that all slaves brought into Brazil should be free; that all persons concerned in the slave trade should be liable to fine and corporal punishment; and that slave ships should be confiscated; and in 1832 he further decreed, that all ships arriving at Rio, should undergo search and examination, in order to the due enforcement of the decree of 1831.

In the year 1826, Mexico bound herself to co-operate with Great Britain for the total abolition of the slave trade; and all the Republics of South America, which when asserting and maintaining their own right to freedom and independence, had abolished slavery—declared, some at one time and some at another, their hostility to the trade in all its branches, and their desire for its suppression.*

---

* The different treaties to which we have referred, may be divided into three classes; the first class gives to each party a mutual right of search of the merchant vessels of the other party within certain geographical limits; and a right of detention of such merchant vessels, as may be found either with slaves on board, or equipped for the slave trade; and these treaties define what circumstances of a vessel, shall constitute, *prima facie*, an equipment for the slave trade. These treaties constitute also Mixed Courts, composed of commissioners of each nation. . . . . Such are the treaties Great Britain has with the Netherlands, Sweden, Brazil, Spain, Portugal, the Argentine Confederation, and with the Republics of Uruguay, of Bolivia, of Chili, and of the Equator.

The second class, are treaties by which a mutual right of search, is, in like manner, as in the first class, granted within specified geographical limits, together with the right of detention, under similar circumstances; but by this second class of treaties, a captured vessel, instead of being tried before a mixed Court of Commission, composed of Judges of the two nations, is handed over to the tribunals of the country under whose flag she has been captured. Such are the treaties Great Britain has with Denmark, Sardinia, the Hanse Towns, Tuscany, the Two Sicilies, Hayti, Venezuela, Mexico, Austria, Russia and Prussia. The third class gives no mutual right of search, but each party engages to maintain a certain force upon the coast of Africa, for the purpose of watching its own merchant flag, and preventing any vessels under that flag from being employed in the prosecution of the slave trade. Such are the treaties with France and the United States.

Thus every civilized nation in Europe and America, whether maritime or not immediately interested in transmarine commerce, has denounced the slave trade as iniquitous, interdicted its subjects, under the severest penalties, from engaging in it; and avowed its willingness or determination to suppress a traffic, stigmatized by them all as deserving the scorn and detestation of every friend of the human race.

As a means of breaking up the trade, of preventing the flags of their respective nations from being prostituted by those engaged in it, and for bringing those to punishment who might be detected in its prosecution, treaties were entered into between Great Britain and France, in the years 1831 and 1833, by which the mutual right of search, of the vessels carrying the flags of those powers respectively, is conceded, within certain geographical limits. To the stipulations of these treaties, almost every maritime power of Europe and America has acceded, except the United States, and may be said to have thus united in a universal league for the extinction of this traffic, which by the municipal laws of some of them, is declared to be piracy, and those detected in its prosecution to be worthy of death.

But notwithstanding the universal verdict of Christendom of the heinous guilt of the African slave trade; the stringent and comprehensive laws that have been enacted by all civilized governments, for the detection and punishment of those who still dare to pursue it, and the vast power employed for carrying these laws into effect, yet the lust of gold, and the hope of escaping detection, have so far proved too strong to be much restrained thereby; and unprincipled and abandoned men, of nearly all nations are still to be found, willing to embark in this illicit commerce; and for the sake of the wealth that they hope to reap, voluntarily make themselves agents in inflicting indescribable misery on their fellow men, and in ensuring their own hopeless degradation. It is true, that there are no parts of the western world, (to supply the supposed wants of which the trade was commenced and carried on for so many years by all maritime powers,) into which slaves can now be legally imported; and but few where the illicit trade is winked at or tolerated by the local authorities. Guiana, the English, French, Dutch, Swedish and Danish possessions in the West Indies, no longer permit an African slave to be landed on their shores; although the French Government, until the year 1848, continued the practice of purchasing slaves, for the purpose of recruiting their army at Senegal on the coast of Africa, and at Demerara; and the Dutch are still guilty of pursuing the same course, in order to keep up their force at Surinam and in Java. But Brazil and the Spanish Islands of Cuba and Porto Rico, in America, and the Islands of Cape Verde, of St. Thomas, and Princes belonging to Portugal on the coast of Africa; though, as we have before said, bound by the treaties of their governments to repudiate and punish the introduction of slaves from a foreign country, nevertheless wink at the illicit traffic, and hold out temptations to slave dealers to run all risks, in order to avail themselves of the gains to be derived from the markets for human flesh, which they covertly maintain.

The flags of Sardinia, Portugal, Brazil, and the United States, are those almost exclusively employed by these outlaws of the civilized world, who seek to conceal their vile employment, and screen themselves from punishment, by the use of one or the other of these flags, as they may deem it most likely to effect their purpose.

Although it is impossible to arrive at any precise knowledge of the number of men, women and children, who are thus torn from their native country, and consigned to hopeless exile and the most cruel bondage; yet facts which are notorious and incontestible, enable us to approximate to the truth, and clearly prove the horrors attending the prosecution of this revolting contraband traffic.

In the year 1839, a work was prepared and published by T. Fowell Buxton, in which he shows from information transmitted to the British Government from reliable sources, that at that time not less than 150,000 persons were annually transported from Africa across the Atlantic, to supply the slave markets of the western world; and 50,000 more were carried off to meet the demands of the Mohammedan slave dealers of Morocco, Tunis, Tripoli, Egypt, Turkey, Persia, Arabia, and the borders of Asia; making a total of 200,000 victims, drained from that unhappy country in the course of a year. It is also demonstrated, that the seizure, march, and detention on the coast, of the poor Africans, are attended with a mortality of 100 per cent.; the middle passage, including the return of those who may be captured by the cruizers, with a mortality of 25 per cent; and the landing and seasoning of those who arrive at the place of their bondage, with a mortality of 20 per cent; thus proving a mortality in the whole process of 145 per cent; "so that for every 1000 negroes alive at the end of the year after their deportation, and available to the planter," there have been sacrificed 1450. It follows of course, that the vessels from which the 150,000 Africans were landed in Brazil, Cuba, and other slave marts of the Christian world, must have had 187,500 on board when they left the coast of Africa, and 37,500 perished in the passage; and before 187,000 were embarked, an equal number, that is 187,000 of their fellow countrymen had fallen victims to the barbarities inflicted on them. Twenty per cent. loss on the 150,000 landed, during their landing and seasoning, gives a further sacrifice of 30,000 lives, so that the annual victims of the slave trade, carried on at that time by professing Christians, according to this work, amounted to 375,000.

There can be no doubt that the number of persons exported from Africa has been materially diminished, perhaps nearly or quite one-half, since the period to which T. F. Buxton's work refers, but within the last two or three years, the African slave trade has again greatly increased, and the whole testimony of those conversant with it, proves indisputably, that the cruelties and mortality still attendant upon it, are little if any less than in the days of its greatest extent.

1840.

We will now proceed to give a brief history of the Slave trade, from the year 1840 to the present time. In the year

1840 it was carried on with more or less activity along the western coast of Africa, from a point immediately below the Great Desert, in the 20th degree of north latitude, to Little Fish Bay, in about the 16th degree of south latitude. As the African coast between these two points crosses not only 36 degrees of latitude, but nearly 30 degrees of longitude, the distance along the sea board must be more than 3500 miles. Along this part of the coast there were a few places, from which, owing to natural impediments, or from obstacles raised against it by men, the slave trade was excluded. At the English settlements of Gambia and Sierra Leone, and that part of Liberia immediately around Monrovia, the opposition of the government and the settlers, was a sufficient bar to the traffic; along a considerable part of the Bight of Benin, there were large tracts of coast so covered with swamp, and a thick growth of mangrove, as to render the trade there impossible; and just north of Little Fish Bay, for 140 miles, a high cliff, lifting a perpendicular breastwork to the sea, as effectually protected that portion of the land from this polluting commerce. The Barracoons, as the buildings are called in which the slaves are confined who are brought to the coast for shipment, were generally located on the rivers in the neighbourhood of some of the European settlements, or of the small trading towns where the native chiefs or kings reside.

The slaves obtained from the coast immediately south of the Great Desert, were principally carried in small trading vessels, a few at a time, to the Cape Verde Islands, where a large number were landed every year. The northernmost islands of this group were supplied principally from the neighbourhood of the French settlements of Senegal and Goree, whilst the southern ones obtained their cargoes from Bissao and Gallinas. These slaves were carried to the Cape Verde, in order that they might be shipped to Cuba or Brazil, with little fear to the slaver, of English scrutiny.—*Class B*, 1841, *page* 534.—*Class B*, 1840, *page* 89.

From Goree southward to Sierra Leone, the trade was actively carried on, yet it was this year somewhat checked at the Island of Corusco, by the destruction of its slave factories. The slave traders located at that place, manifested their antipathy to the opposers of the trade, by firing on the boats of an English man-of-war. This wanton act of aggression was quickly retaliated. Their buildings, with the merchandize contained in them, were destroyed, and the traders being left without the means of carrying on the traffic, it was for a time much depressed.—*Class A*, 1841, *p*. 9.—*Class A*, 1841, *p*. 10.

From Rio Nunez, that famous mart for slaves, but few were carried away by sea this year, the slave traders preferring to take in their cargoes from the neighbouring port of Bissao, from which about 2000 slaves were annually taken, principally to Cuba.—*Class A*, 1841, *p*. 9, 10.

At Rio Pongas, the number shipped had materially decreased, in consequence of the negro collectors of slaves not keeping good faith with the masters of the slavers. In many instances, after having obtained possession of the goods sent to pay for the intended living cargo, they neglected to furnish the slaves, or did it after a long, and to the interest of the ship owner, a ruinous delay.

The trade was brisk in many places between Sierra Leone and Cape Palmas; Liberia at that time protecting a very small portion of the coast from this traffic. From the 5th month to the end of the year, 21 vessels sailed for Gallinas to obtain cargoes of slaves. Of these, 15 were captured, and one being driven from its intended port by British cruizers, put into Sierra Leone, where it was seized and condemned. The remaining five succeeded in carrying off 1560 slaves.* The slave factories at this place being destroyed, the native King gave 841 slaves, which were found in them, to the English, who carried them to Sierra Leone, where they were free. The destruction of these factories took place in the 11th month of this year. They were eight in number, very extensive, and gave employment to sixty white men. During the nine months immediately preceding their destruction, 1000 tons of goods, to be employed

* Class A, 1841, page 9, Correspondence with the British Commissioners relating to the slave trade.

exclusively in the purchase of slaves, had been landed at them. Ten thousand slaves had been annually shipped from this station.—(*Class A*, 1841, *p*. 10.) The attack on these factories was occasioned by the discovery, that a number of the English Sierra Leone subjects had been seized by the Gallinas traders and sold into slavery.

The English ships of war, which during this year were stationed about the Gulf of Guinea, occasioned the number of slaves shipped from Lagos and Whydah, to be very much below the average of former years. The port of Ambriz was so closely watched by these cruizers for three months, that no slave vessel could approach it, and during the whole of this time 2000 slaves collected there for shipment, were maintained at a heavy expense to the traders. (*Class A*, 1841, *p*. 8.) From Loanda and its neighbourhood many cargoes of slaves were taken, although the Portuguese governor at that place offered some obstruction to the traffic, seizing and liberating a number of poor captives brought there for sale. South of Loanda, the principal mart for slaves was Benguela, although almost every where along that coast slave ships could obtain cargoes.

On the eastern coast of Africa, many slaves were shipped from Quillimane, Inhambo, Iboo and Delgoa Bay, and even from the neighbourhood of Mozambique; although Marinha, the Portuguese governor in that place, incited by recent instructions from his government at home, exerted himself to suppress the traffic. About the middle of 1840, he seized one Spanish brig, and two Portuguese ships, which had come for slaves to that port. This vigorous act was felt as a severe blow by the slave collectors, who had at that time 2500 poor victims gathered in the neighbourhood of Mozambique, intended for these three vessels.—*Class B*, 1841, *p*. 468, 469, 471.

The slave trade had been openly carried on from all the Portuguese African settlements, until the close of the year 1836, when, as before stated, the government in Portugal issued a decree, forbidding the traffic. Previous to that time, a fixed sum was received at the custom house in every port, for each slave shipped, and the government derived considerable revenue from this source. The governors in these possessions received a small salary from Portugal, which was paid them in a coarse cloth, much used in the purchase of slaves. It was on the fees which the governors received from the slave traders, that they principally depended for support, and these were sufficient to enable them to maintain the style of living expected from their station, and to realize considerable estates.—*Class A.*, 1844, *p.* 312, &c.

In 1840 the slave trade still continued to be carried on in all the Portuguese settlements; and though the governors in some of them endeavoured to suppress what had now become an illegal traffic; yet, having little means of enforcing their commands, their subjects easily thwarted them. Some of the governors continued openly to encourage the trade, and the slave traders. Ferdinando Cartes de Costa, of Quillimane, was one of these. For his patronage and support in this contraband trade, he received large bribes, amounting in one instance to $7000 on a single cargo. The trade in the neighbourhood of that port was systematized and carried on in the most perfect manner. Persons resident in Quillimane were employed as factors to purchase slaves, and they made use of native traders, to collect them throughout the country. The factors supplied the merchandize, which alone passes for money in the interior, to their black agents, who with it paid for their unhappy brethren, who were to be torn from their native country and sent to hopeless bondage in a foreign land. As fast as the slaves were brought to Quillimane, they were branded, and committed to the charge of free blacks, who had land granted them in the neighbourhood, on the sole condition that they should receive and take care of the slaves until the time of embarkation. Sometimes two or three hundred would be collected at one of these depots; and they were employed as labourers on the farms of those who had charge of them. When the vessel arrived in which they were to be shipped, it generally came into port, gave or received notice, from which barracoon it was to take in its cargo, and then stood out to sea again, where it remained until the time for shipping the cargo had arrived. The factors in the mean while busied themselves in collecting from the various depots, the requisite number of slaves to the assigned barracoon, of which there were several both north and south of the port. At the time appointed, the ship came to anchor near by, and through the active aid of a large number of men and boats, a cargo of several hundred was taken on board, and packed away in the hold in a few hours. It often happened, that before night of the day in which the ship first commenced loading, she was at sea with her cargo, stretching far south to give a wide berth to the Cape of Good Hope, lest she should fall in with the British cruizers.—*Class A*, 1844, *p.*312.

We have already stated, that the principal places in the new world, to which slaves are carried from Africa, are the Brazilian Territories and the Spanish Islands. The number of slaves landed along the coast of Brazil, in 1840, according to the official table of statistics laid before the Parliament of Great Britain, was 30,000, and in Cuba and the neighbouring islands belonging to Spain, 14,470. The reason of the diminution of the trade from 1839, when the number landed in Brazil was 42,182, was probably owing, in great measure, to the increased activity of the British cruizers. Many slave vessels, during the year, returned in ballast to the places from which they had sailed, finding the African ports where they were destined, so closely watched, they were unable to secure their cargoes.

It was from no want of demand for the slaves in Cuba or Brazil, nor from any disposition in those who had heretofore made immmense fortunes at the traffic, to engage in lawful commerce. Slaves brought as great prices as heretofore, and from Cuba great efforts to extend the trade were made. This is manifested by the number of slave vessels from that Island, captured during this year. Of 28 vessels condemned at Sierra Leone, 20 were engaged in the Cuban trade, and 8 only in that to Brazil. Had those from Cuba been suffered to pursue their employment without interruption, they would probably have made more than one trip each, and the number landed on that island would doubtless have been more than doubled. The

2

Cuban vessels, obtaining their slaves almost entirely on that part of the western coast of Africa, extending from Sierra Leone down by Cape Palmas, and along the northern shore of the Gulf of Guinea, they were brought more frequently under notice of the British cruizers than those of Brazil, engaged in the same unlawful commerce. All the slaves taken from Quillimane and other ports on the east coast of Africa, for the "American market," appear to have been carried to Brazil. Of the 28 slave vessels captured by the English, 11 were to obtain cargoes from various parts of the coast between Sierra Leone to Cape Palmas; 8 from the barracoons in the Bight of Benin; 2 from the River Gaboon, just south of the Bight of Biafra, and 6 from ports south of the equator. Only 3 of these vessels had shipped any slaves when they were captured, and the number in the 3 was but 720.—*Class A*, 1841, *page* 8.

As it was known that the flag of the United States protected the vessel bearing it, from the right of search by any cruizer of a foreign power, that flag had been carried by many Spanish and Portuguese vessels bound to Africa for slaves. In the year 1836, five vessels left Cuba, under the "stripes and stars," for Africa; in 1837, 11; in 1838, 19; in 1839 the number was 23; while in 1840 there were but 9. This reduction was doubtless occasioned by the seizure of a number of such vessels by British cruizers, and their condemnation at Sierra Leone, as Spanish, Portuguese, or Brazilian property, by the sending some for adjudication to the United States, and by the increased activity of the national vessels of the United States, on the African coast, in their endeavours to suppress the slave trade. Americans have since been quite as much connected with this infamous traffic as ever, but their national flag has not been so openly used by foreigners to cover it.—*Class A*, 1841, *pages* 171, 172.

Of the 28 cargoes of slaves landed this year in Cuba, all except two or three were taken there in vessels bearing the Portuguese flag. A number of the vessels had, however, sailed from that island under the flag of the United States. Two Spanish vessels in the Cuban slave trade, were captured by

British cruizers, and taken to Havana for adjudication; and, one in attempting to escape, was driven on a reef and completely wrecked. This last vessel had been most successful in her iniquitous employment. The name under which she first sailed was "Urraca:"—

She landed on Cuba	1 cargo of slaves in		1830
"	2	"	1831
"	1	"	1832
"	2	"	1833
"	1	"	1834
"	1	"	1836

About the close of 1836 she was transferred at the Cape Verdes to a Portuguese owner, and sailed from thence as the "Arrogante." Under this name she made one successful trip, but on the second was captured by a British cruizer, and condemned at Sierra Leone. Her original Spanish owner, by an agent, purchased her at public sale in that port, and her name being changed to "Iberia," she was immediately sent for a fresh cargo, which she landed safely at Havana. She had cleared again for Africa, when being chased by a British cruizer, her captain finding she could not escape, run her on the reef where she was destroyed. She had landed not less than 4000 slaves on the Spanish Islands, in her ten successful voyages.—*Class A*, 1841, *p.* 173.—*Class B*, 1840, *p.* 57.

One of the captured vessels brought into Havana this year was named the "Jesus Maria," and had on board 252 negroes, mostly boys and girls. The average age of this cargo, was thought by the British officers who examined them, not to exceed 11 years. The vessel was very small, measuring but 35 tons. She had been long employed in trade from the Cape Verde Islands to the African coast, principally in carrying provisions. Finding on his last trip to the coast that he could obtain a cargo of slaves, the captain, although his vessel was not prepared as a slaver, and had not even the usual accommodations, yet crowded into her diminutive hold, 278 negroes. The vessel was badly provided for a voyage across the Atlantic; she had no spare anchor, or boat, was old and leaky, and if she had encountered storms, it was the opinion of her captors she must inevitably have foundered. Previous to the capture of the vessel, 26 of the slaves had perished, some, at least, through the effect of gross abuse, 12 more died before they reached Havana, and many others soon afterwards, of weakness and disease engendered by the crowded condition of the hold in which they had been confined.

Commander Stewart, who captured the vessel, thus writes to the English Commissioner Kennedy, at Havana, of this vessel. "The negroes are dreadfully crowded; several of them are in a very emaciated condition, and it is of infinite importance they should be removed out of the vessel without a moment's loss of time. If they are detained on board to await her condemnation, more wretched victims will be added to the list of those already dead. When I fell in with her she was short of water, which I believe is one of the causes of so many deaths. I therefore took her to an anchorage off the west end of Santa Cruz, supplied her with water, provisions, and a few things for the sick children. The negroes, with the exception of four women, are all children, their average age from 10 to 15. The vessel being a slow sailer, I have towed her as far as Cape Francois, from whence she is certain to carry a fair wind and smooth water to Havana. I regret my orders will not permit me to take her there myself. She is the most miserable craft I ever saw in the shape of a slaver; is not above 35 tons, has no boat, anchor, cable, spare sails, stores, not even a few planks for the negroes to lay upon." *Class A*, 1841, *p.* 178, 179.

Much gross abuse and wickedness had been inflicted on these poor young victims during the voyage, whilst they were at the mercy of the slave captain and his crew. Indeed, the facts elicited by an examination of the survivors are too horrible and offensive to narrate. The captain, obviously afraid of a public examination into his conduct, seized an opportunity when the vessel reached the harbour of Havana to jump overboard, and swimming to shore, escaped. Here we have one instance of the legitimate effects of the slave trade. The placing defenceless men and unprotected women, at the mercy of cruel, passionate and wicked men, must ever give birth to injury, oppression and outrage.—*Class B*, 1841, *page* 81–85.

The general feeling of the people of Cuba favoured the continuance of the slave trade. Some indeed of the old planters, who had as many slaves as they desired, would have been willing to see the trade suppressed, for this would have raised the value of the slaves on their estates. There were however, many new coffee and sugar plantations starting on the island, the owners of which, some of whom were citizens of the United States, strongly countenanced the traffic. These wished rapidly to increase the number of their slaves, and desired to do it at as small a price as they could. The sugar exported from Cuba had recently been sold to great profit, and the amount of it had doubled in the preceding five years. This had given rise to much pecuniary prosperity in the island. Havana, and the other chief cities, had greatly increased in population, and many large towns had sprung into existence. More labourers were demanded for the work doing, and about to be done, on the island, and most of the inhabitants looked only to Africa for them. It is true, a few of the planters sought for free labourers, and some white persons from Catalan, and many others from the Canary Islands were employed by them on their sugar estates. This was as yet an experiment.—*Class A*, 1841, *pages* 167–171.

In illustration of the profits accruing at that time on a full cargo of slaves, we may state on the authority of an American officer in a communication to the Navy Department of the United States, that the slaver Venus, an American vessel, carried from the Gallinas a cargo of 800 slaves, which were sold in Cuba at so high a price as to realize more than $200,000 profit, after paying for the vessel and all expenses.—*Class D*, 1840, *page* 92.

Of the 30,000 slaves carried this year to Brazil, nearly all were landed on the coast at some distance from any port of entry. After parting with her living cargo, the slaver would bear away for Rio Janeiro, Bahia, Pernambuco, Maranham, Para, Ciara, or some place of less consequence, where she would refit, and from whence she would again clear out to the coast of Africa. We have stated, that the republics of South America had abolished the slave trade, yet some of those vessels which left Rio on this errand, took out a clearance for Montevideo, in Uruguay, where the slave merchants of Rio had regular correspondents who despatched the vessel to some part of the slave coast. We have already said, that many of the slaves brought to Brazil, were from the eastern coast of Africa. The relative numbers generally we cannot tell, but of those landed near Rio during the last five months of 1839, we have information.

Six vessels bringing 2974 were from Quillemane, one which landed 450 from Mozambique,—making 3424 from the eastern coast,—five bringing 1234, obtained their cargoes at Angola, two with 638 were from Benguela, and one with 370 from the river Zaire or Congo, being in all 2242, from the western coast.—*Class B, page* 143.

Beside those sent exclusively for slaves, most of the Brazilian trading vessels to the coast of Africa or adjacent islands, were prepared to ship 50 or 60 negroes in addition to their lawful cargo. The whole number of vessels which sailed for Africa from Brazil in 1840, was 78. Of these 44 cleared out under the Brazilian flag, 27 under the Portuguese, 3 under that of the United States, 1 under the English, 2 under French, and 1 under the Sardinian. Those which bore the flag of the United States had been remarkably successful as slavers. Of the 46 which came to Brazil from Africa during the year, 15 bore the Brazilian flag, 23 the Portuguese, 3 that of the United States, 2 the Sardinian, 1 the French, 1 the Danish, and 1 the Belgian.—*Class A*, 1840,—Rio de Janiero.—*Class B*, 1840, *Brazil, &c.*

Two slave vessels captured with full cargoes were brought to Rio for adjudication during this year, one from Benguela had 280 negroes on board, and as she measured but 56 tons she was of course crowded. The other was a canoe forty feet long, and had 47 slaves in her.

The decree of the Emperor of Brazil issued in 1831, to which we have already referred, declaring that all Africans imported into that country thereafter should be free, had always been to a great extent null, because the will of the community was opposed to its enforcement. Many of the inhabitants of Brazil were however dissatisfied with its remaining, impotent as it was, on the statute book, and early in 1840, strong efforts were made for its repeal. They however failed.

The principal participation of the French government in the slave trade during the year 1840, appears to have been the purchase on behalf of the government of a few hundred black men to recruit the army at Senegal and Goree. These slaves were nominally made free upon being incorporated into the army, and their condition was probably not much worse than that of French conscripts generally, who are torn from all the endearments of home, and held to military service by the fear of an ignominious death on desertion.—*Class C*, 1840, *France.*

Portugal was deeply concerned in the Slave trade, and the vessels and capital of her citizens were actively engaged in it. We have already said, that in her Cape de Verde Islands there were depots for the collection of the slaves, which were taken there in small numbers from Africa, that they might be securely shipped to the market which the western world offered for them. The Spanish Canary Islands were made use of, by those engaged in the Slave trade, as depots, but not to the same extent as the Cape Verde, which are much nearer that portion of the African coast from which slaves could be obtained.

The English government, finding that the Dutch were in the habit of filling the vacancies in their military forces at Surinam and Java, with slaves purchased for that purpose in Africa, called the consideration of the King of the Netherlands this year to the subject, as well as to the fact, that the authorities at the Dutch settlement of St. George D' Elmina, on the gold coast, furnished or permitted others to furnish, slaves to the Brazilian ships.—*Class B*, 1840, *Netherlands.*

About the conclusion of the year 1839, the Pope had issued a Brief against the Slave trade, which the English government took great pains to have printed and distributed in countries where the Catholic religion prevailed. The Captain General of Cuba, refused to allow the publication of this Brief in the papers of Havana, and the Spanish government sustained him in this act. The fear that this Brief, if published, would operate to intimidate superstitious believers in the Pope's power, and might render ecclesiastics severe on such as violated it, when they came to confession, appears to have been the reason why the Captain General did not desire to see it spread in Cuba.*—*Class B.* 1840, *p.* 12.

Thus popish Spain endeavoured to neutralize the efforts of the Romish Pontiff against slavery. Indeed, from the whole tenor of the actions of the government of Spain, during this year, it is evident that whilst it did not deem it prudent to revoke the former agreements with Great Britain against the Slave trade, it intended quietly to allow its subjects to violate those agreements at their will. The effect of the publication of the Pope's Brief at Brazil, was salutary in a few instances. One ecclesiastic at least, deemed himself conscientiously restrained by it, from granting absolution to those engaged in the Slave trade. This was considered a terrible blow, by men who believed that a priestly ordination gave authority to man to grant pardon at will for sin.

Along the northern coast of Africa, many slaves continued to be brought for sale. Tripoli was, in 1840, perhaps the principal depot, there being about 3000 annually sold from thence. The slave caravans, to that place, from Ghandames and Timbuctoo, have a long and tedious journey across the Sandy Deserts, in which many of their slaves die. On ap-

* The minister of Spain, in London, offered political reasons against allowing its public promulgation throughout the Spanish territories. He says, "the Kings of Spain fearing that, *under the shadow of religion*, the jurisdiction and royal rights of the crown might be usurped, to the detriment of the supreme power of the nation, and of the public tranquility, have managed, for centuries past, with incessant vigilance and vigour to restrain, within just limits, the *pretensions* of Rome; and as maxims and doctrines contrary to the royal power, might be inserted in the Pontifical Decrees canonically issued, the Crown of Spain has always opposed itself to the reception into the Kingdom of any Bull from the Roman Curia, which *has not been asked for*, and which does not come through the channel of the Ambassador or Agents of Her Majesty."

proaching Tripoli, the Shieks, who rule outside of the city, expect to receive one slave of every four brought for sale. When this tribute is not peaceably paid, they attack the caravan and appropriate all to themselves.—*Class D, p.* 19.

The Slave trade was very extensively carried on in Egypt, partly to furnish labourers, but principally to fill the army and the harems there. In addition to those brought in on private account, the government was wont to send detachments of the army into the nearest negro districts to recruit their own ranks by force. On the eastern coast of Africa, north of the Portuguese territory, the principal part of the Slave trade was in the hands of the Imaum of Muscat, whose African Territories were over 1100 miles in extent, and the greater part of whose revenue was derived from the sale of slaves. From 11,000 to 15,000 were sold annually in his dominions, being partly negroes, and partly Abyssinians.—*Class D*, 1842, *p.* 68.

There were several marts for slaves about the entrance to the Red Sea, from which a considerable trade to Arabia, and to ports on the Persian Gulf was carried on. At one of these ports, Burburra, a fair is held, to which forty or fifty vessels from different places go to trade; few if any of which, ever go away without taking slaves. Very many of the slaves thus carried out of Africa, are Christians, principally Abyssinian children. The fierce Galla tribes, located along the south border of Abyssinia, are ever at war with it, or at least are continually making predatory excursions into it,—burning its villages, and seizing as slaves all its inhabitants who have not perished in the conflict. Many of the men and women are kept by the Gallas for their own service, but the children are generally sold to traders, who take them to the Red Sea ports, where they are purchased for the eastern market. Many of them have found their way into the harems of the East Indies. The children thus sold are from eight to sixteen years of age. Of those carried across into Arabia, from two to three hundred a month were brought to Mocha, where, Captain Harris* says, " on land-

* Class Book A, 1843, p. 436–455.

ing they were immediately placed within a pound unclothed, from whence they were driven to a well for water twice a day like a flock of sheep." From the information obtained by investigations entered into by the English government and the East India Company, it appears that many young women, not slaves, were induced to go, under promise of marriage with seamen, from Burburra and other places; and, after being treated as wives, were sold at the first good market as slaves. The Arabian subjects of the Imaum of Muscat, all hold slaves,—at least as soon as they can earn enough to purchase one, they do it. The meanest in esteem or rank amongst them, the poorest in estate, will do no sort of bodily labour after he has become possessed of a slave. He trusts to that slave to earn or steal enough for his subsistence, as well as to enable him to purchase young girls for his harem. The number of slaves taken annually from Africa, for the supply of Mahommedan and Pagan countries, has been variously estimated at from 75,000 to 120,000.—[See many more particulars of this trade, *Class A*, 1843, *p*. 358–460.

From the United States of North America in 1840, slaves direct from Africa were legally excluded. Mexico had abolished slavery, and thereby cut off all demand for slaves. Guatimala, or Central America, had in 1824 passed a law, forever abolishing slavery. New Grenada received no negroes from Africa after the year 1834, and though a few were brought into her territory by planters removing there, the whole number of slaves was on the decrease. By law all children of slaves born after 1821, were free at 13 years of age, and a portion of the estates of all who die is set apart for the purchase of slaves for manumission. Slavery in Venezuela was on the decline, her laws concerning slavery as well as those of the Republic of Equator, closely resembling those of New Grenada. Peru had abolished the slave trade, and Bolivia in the ninth month, 1840, entered into a treaty with Great Britain for the abolition of the traffic in slaves, and admitted none but freemen to enter her territories. Chile had taken an early step against slavery, declaring in 1811, that all the children born of slaves, henceforward should be free. In the year 1823 all slaves were by a decree of the conservative senate, liberated from bondage, and the constitution of the country declares that any slave touching her soil is free. In 1839 she entered into a treaty with Great Britain for the abolition of the slave trade to Africa. Buenos Ayres, in 1813, abolished the traffic in slaves; and in 1840 slavery had almost become extinct in the territory. In Uruguay, or Montevideo, acts had been passed many years against slavery, and in 1839, she as well as Buenos Ayres, entered into treaties with Great Britain against the slave trade.

[*See Class D, under head of the above named States.*]

1841.

During the year 1841, 22 vessels captured whilst engaged in the slave trade, were condemned at Sierra Leone. Of these, 10 were to have carried slaves to the Spanish West India Islands, and 12 to Brazil. The cargoes for six of them were to be obtained north of Cape Palmas, 7 at the ports on the Bights of Benin and Biafra, in the Gulf of Guinea, and nine at slave stations south of the Equator. One of the vessels, the Josephine of Havana, had on board at the time of her capture, 291 fine healthy slaves, all of whom were males. She had taken her cargo in at Whydah in two hours, and remained in the port but four hours, during which time she did not come to anchor.—*Class A,* 1842, *pages* 3 *to* 7, *and Class A,* 1841, *pages* 84 *and* 85.

Among the interesting incidents, illustrating the evils to which the existence of slavery gives birth, narrated in the proceedings for 1841, is the following. A trader of Rio Pongos, being about to take some slaves to Havana, prevailed on two free coloured persons to accompany him. One of them was named Christopher Weatherhead. He was a mulatto, the son of an English trader. The other one named Mory, was a near connection of one of the Rio Pongos chiefs. They arrived safely at Havana, where the trader with whom they went, having by his extravagance squandered his property, accepted the command of an English brig bound to Charleston, South Carolina, the captain of which had died. At his request his two companions from Africa went with him to the shores of North America. Whilst at Charleston, the new captain again gave way to habits which brought on pecuniary difficulties, and to raise money, he enticed his coloured friends on shore, and sold them as slaves. The two captives determined that they would not work as slaves, and this determination they maintained. The person who had purchased them, finding that all the punishment inflicted on them, failed to subdue them, sold them to a second planter, and he meeting with the same success, soon parted with them to a third. This last owner, on being informed that his new slaves would not work, whatever force or punishment was applied to them, examined them himself, as to the cause. In reply to his questions they informed him the manner of their being brought from Africa, and the fraudulent means by which a pretended sale had been made of them. This planter was a humane man, and though he had given $1500 for them, he immediately interested himself in investigating the truth of their assertions. He wrote to Africa to the parties to whom they referred, as capable of testifying what was the real nature of their condition in life. Finding from the answer received, that their narrative was true, he set them at liberty, and they returned in safety to the land of their birth.—*Class A*, 1841, *pages* 29, 30.

The number of slaves landed this year, 1841, in Cuba, is estimated at 11,857.* These all came in vessels under the Portuguese flag, although some of them were doubtless Spanish property. They had been brought from African ports north of the Equator, and the Cape Verde Islands.

In the third month of this year, a new Captain General for Cuba, arrived at Havana,—Geronimo Valdes. Although not in all things a bold and open opposer of slavery, he yet did much more than his predecessor in discouraging the Slave trade.—*Class A*, 1841, *p.* 204, *&c.*

The regular fees which had been paid per head, on landing fresh slaves in Havana, had been,—to the governor, $16; to the senior officer of the Spanish naval force, $4; to the collector of the customs, $7, and to the Gen-d'arme who guarded them, 50 cents. The whole fees being $27 50 for each slave. Captain

* Report to Parliament 1849.

Tucker, of the English navy, captured a vessel of one hundred and five tons burden, which had in her former trips paid the owners for her cost and all expenses. At the time of capture, she was prepared for a cargo of four hundred. These would have brought, at the low estimate of $300 a head, $120,000. Captain Tucker gives an account of the cost to the owner, of delivering such a cargo in Havana.—

The first cost of 400 slaves in Africa $16, -	$6,400
Fees at Havana, 400 at $27 50 - - -	11,000
The Captain, $600 salary and 10 per cent. commission	12,600
The 1st. Pilot, $420 salary and $3\frac{1}{2}$ per cent. "	4,620
The 2d. Pilot, $360 salary and 1 per cent. "	1,560
The Boatswain, 360 salary and 1 per cent. "	1,560
The Carpenter - - - - - - -	300
The Cooper - - - - - - - -	300
The Cook - - - - - - - -	240
The Steward - - - - - - - -	240
Fifteen Seamen, at $180 - - - - - -	2,700
Provisions, Harbour-fees, &c. - - - - -	3,380
The total cost of the slaves to the owner of the vessel	$44,900

This leaves a profit of $75,100 on the voyage.—*Class B*, 1841, *pages* 3–5.

Whilst the trade offered such pecuniary inducements to unprincipled men, who can wonder that they continued to carry it on,—and whilst the governor of Cuba cared more for the treasures of earth, than for the claims of justice and humanity, it is not strange that he winked at the traffic, when the cargo of one single vessel would have paid him $6,400. Very many cargoes were landed, consisting of from 700 to 1000 persons.

We have reason to believe that Valdes refused in any way to partake of the gain of oppression,—at least, the advocates of slavery felt that he was opposed to them, and the friends of liberty on the Island began to declare themselves. Soon after his arrival, some of the creole inhabitants presented a memorial against the Slave trade. This memorial shows that they feared the ultimate consequences which might result to the Island, if the constant influx of slaves were not stopped. They cast their eyes around them,—they beheld warlike Hayti, with 900,000 blacks; Jamaica with 400,000; the Bahama Islands with 12,000, and they asked themselves the question, What would be the issue in some future day, if these blacks should attack them and incite their slaves to revolt. Already the slaves numbered sixty per cent. of the inhabitants. They thought it would be the part of wisdom to prepare for such an event, by diminishing the black population and increasing the white,—by encouraging white labourers from foreign countries to emigrate there. The memorial referring to one estate, on which free white labourers were introduced, says—"Already in the central portion of the Island, the glorious career of agricultural reform has been opened by a son of our illustrious Catalonia. He, however, and all who follow his excellent example, must expect to have to struggle for some time to come, with the innumerable obstacles which habit, prejudice, bad faith, and above all, the deleterious influence of the Slave trade, will oppose to them; for it is in that traffic alone, that we are to seek for the origin of all the evils by which we are assailed."—*Class B*, 1841, *p.* 263–5.

The general expression of the English people of their abhorrence of the Slave trade and slavery, and its repetition by many others in Europe, began to be felt even in Madrid. One of the newspapers in that city, fearlessly denounced the traffic in slaves and the keeping human beings in unconditional bondage. This paper being in regular course transmitted to Cuba and circulated there, produced no little excitement amongst the partisans of slavery and the Slave trade on the Island. They proceeded to put forth various documents in favour of slavery, condemning the Madrid papers,—and all Englishmen in general, and the Consul of that nation who resided at Havana in particular. They asserted that slavery in Cuba was better than freedom in Africa.—*Class B*, 1841, *p.* 286, 7.

The excitement in Cuba was largely increased by the proposition to call a convention, to ascertain how many slaves had been introduced into the Island, since the Spanish law against the trade had made it a crime to bring them there. These poor slaves were legally free, by laws which Cuba, as a Spanish colony, was bound to obey. The inhabitants, however, were not prepared for such a convention, and there were many plain indications that they intended to fight for their slaves, even against Spain itself, rather than surrender them without full compensation. They admitted that at least 200,000 had been illegally brought in, and it was manifest that the treasury of Spain would prove altogether inadequate to furnish the funds necessary to purchase them of the present holders.—*Class B*, 1841, *p*. 365–387.

Valdes seized a number of newly imported slaves, and by his course of action, appears soon to have lost the confidence of the warm supporters of slavery. During the year, the Segunda Rosario was brought to Havana for adjudication, having been captured by a British vessel. She had 293 slaves on board, which had been obtained at Rio Pongos. The vessel was condemned, and the negroes found in her were carried in British ships to a land of freedom.

The capture of fifteen vessels engaged in the slave trade to Brazil, made a sensible reduction in the number landed in that country during the year. According to the account laid before the British Parliament, there were only 16,000, being but little more than half the number landed in 1840.

Forty-six vessels arrived at Brazil during the year from Africa, most of which were more or less directly engaged in the slave trade, or connected with it. Five of these vessels obtained cargoes north of the Gulf of Guinea, 19 on the Gulf, principally at Angola, 8 south of the Gulf, and one from the eastern coast. Thirteen are noted as from the African coast; the spot or port not designated. Three vessels were captured and carried into Rio; one of these had lost on the voyage, 120 out of 500 negroes shipped, and many more of them died soon after reaching the English store ship at Rio. The survivors of the captured negroes were sent to Demarara, where they were free.—*Class A, and B*, 1841, under head Brazil, &c.

Of the vessels which escaped the cruizers, and landed their

cargoes in Brazil, one had lost 183 out of 683 taken in; and this loss of life chiefly depended on the crowded condition of the vessels, and a scarcity of water and provisions. Of the 500 of this company who were landed, many were very sickly. Another had lost 117 of a cargo of 764, and many perished on the beach after landing. The most remarkable voyage noted in the year, was that of an open launch, which left Africa with 42 slaves, and landed 36 of them safely near Pernambuco.

During the year 1841, Mexico on the western continent, and Russia, Prussia and Austria, on the eastern, entered into further treaties with England, for the suppression of the traffic in slaves. On the coast of Africa on the eleventh of the 1st month, Lieutenant Seagram of the English navy, entered into a treaty with King Freeman, and Prince Freeman, of New Cestos, by which the latter pledged themselves, that the slave trade in the country which owned their sway, was then and forever abolished. This was making one more free spot of land between Liberia and Cape Palmas. On the twenty-third of the 4th month of this year, Henry Vere Huntly, Lieutenant Governor of the British settlement at Gambia, entered into a treaty with the neighbouring king of Cantabar, who pledged himself not to allow any slaves to be sent from his dominions, and placed himself and his country under the protection of the sovereign of Great Britain, that his subjects might be secure from the incursions of neighbouring chiefs. The slave trade was still carried on to and from the Cape Verde Islands, and even Teneriffe; and slaves could be obtained from Bissao and Cacheo; yet during the year, the trade north of Cape Palmas was much reduced. To the French settlement at Casamanca, many slaves were still taken. The native traders took down to the coast a large number, principally males, to carry ivory and heavy goods to the French merchants, and generally desired to sell such a portion of them, as was not needed to carry back the goods received in exchange for the produce brought. When the number of slaves at Casamanca became considerable, they were taken, under the protection of the French government vessels to Senegal, where they were sold at auction to serve for 14 years. At the end of that period they were nominally free, but were compelled to enter the French army, and were sent to the West Indies.—*Class A*, 1841, *pages* 22 and 23.

The slave trade in the Bights of Benin and Biafra, was, although somewhat less than in recent years, still very extensive. On the 7th of the fifth month, Lieutenant Blount made a treaty with King Bell of Bell's town on the Cameroon's River, and with King Acqua of Acqua town on the same stream, by which the slave trade was abolished in the territories of each of these rulers. On the 28th of eighth month, Captain Trotter and his officers made a treaty with Obi Osai, the chief of the Aboh country on the Niger to the same import, and on the 6th of the ninth month a similar one with Ochijah, the Attah of the Egarra country on the same river. On the 6th of twelfth month Lieutenant Blount made an engagement with two of the native kings on Calibar, for the immediate abolition of the slave trade in those parts of the coast of the Bight of Biafra over which they had control.*

To the west of these places the slave trade was still carried on at Attoca, a small dependence of Accra, a Danish settlement. The governor in vain set himself in opposition to the trade; he had not the power effectually to check it. South of the Bight of Biafra, the trade was on the increase, being permitted and encouraged at the Portuguese settlements there.

On the eastern coast of Africa, but little change had been effected during this year. At Mozambique the Portuguese governor continued to oppose the trade, and to seize the slaves brought for shipment, but cargoes of slaves were still obtained freely at Quillimane, and some other places belonging to Portugal. The Imaum of Muscat continued to derive his revenue from the slaves taken from his possessions in Africa. Egypt still filled up her armies with negroes, dragged from their

* See account of all these treaties, in "Instructions for the Guidance of Her Majesty's Naval Officers employed in the suppression of the Slave Trade," pages 90 to 98. The Treaties themselves are in the Appendix to the volume.

wives and families, and supplied her own harems and those of her eastern neighbours with the younger females. From Tripoli many continued to be sent to Constantinople. The sufferings of the slaves brought across the Great Desert to Tripoli, continued to be terribly destructive to human strength and life. This year 300 out of a caravan of 900, perished for want of sufficient food and drink. By a letter from the English Consul at that place, it appears, that up to the 22nd of the sixth month, more thah 2000 had arrived there, and that they were "in a most miserably wretched state."

The Bey of Tunis this year issued a law against the slave trade; set his own slaves at liberty,—prohibited any from being exported,—abolished the slave market in the place, and had the building in which it had been held, destroyed. The king of Greece,—whose subjects had been the principal carriers of slaves from the African ports to Turkish ones—at the instigation of the English government, this year issued a law against the traffic.—*Class D*, 1841.

1842.

In the year 1842, of the nine vessels condemned at Sierra Leone as having been captured whilst engaged in the slave trade, five were Brazilian property, three Spanish, and one Portuguese. The three Spanish were from Cuba, and were bound, one to New Cestos, one to Bissao, and one to Lagos, in the Bight of Benin, for their slaves. The other six were in the Brazil trade. The Portuguese vessel had shipped her cargo, consisting of 450 slaves, at Lagos a day or two before her capture. One of the Brazilian vessels had engaged her cargo at Elmina in the Bight of Benin; one was to take hers at the islands of St. Thomas and Princes further south, one at Congo, and two at Benguela. On examining the survivors of the Africans on board the Portuguese vessel, there were found to be 446. Of these there were males 388; 225 being men, and 163 boys, Of females there were but 58, consisting of 15 women and 43 girls.—*Class A*, 1843, *pages* 2 *to* 6.

The number of slaves landed in Cuba during the year 1842, is estimated at 3150. This diminution was owing partly to the vigilance of the British cruizers, partly to the loss of so many vessels already captured, but mainly to the determined opposition which it was understood the Captain General had made and would make to the traffic. But three vessels cleared out from Havana for the coast of Africa during the year, supposed to be intended for that traffic; nine vessels from the coast arrived, seven under the Portuguese flag and two under the Spanish. One Portuguese vessel was seized and brought into Havana as a prize, and another was seized by the Captain General whilst lying in port. During the year Valdez gave certificates of freedom to 1215 emancipated Africans. These were negroes found on board captured vessels, and entitled to their freedom. They had been worked as slaves for many years, nominally to prepare them for living as freemen. The conduct of the Captain General was such, as to give more and more umbrage to the slave traders of Havana and their supporters throughout Cuba. He seized during the year, 754 negroes, who had been recently brought in from Africa, and declared them free; beside which he issued a new code for the regulation of the conduct of slave masters towards those in servitude to them. This code provides for the slave's proper maintenance and comfort—compels a master, if he has treated one cruelly, to sell him at a minimum price to a new master, chosen by the slave; and finally it provides that slaves shall be set at liberty, or sold as it were to themselves, if they have honestly earned the amount which another person would give for them. The publication of this code created a strong excitement amongst the slave holders, and they began to make strenuous efforts to induce the government of Spain to recall the Captain General. Their efforts proved effectual, and these regulations do not appear to have been observed. It should be remembered, that the 754 negroes above referred to, who were declared free, were yet bound out, or rather sold for a term of years; and that whilst in this condition they were more hardly treated than the slaves themselves. Their employers had less interest in using them well, than they had their slaves, for the latter they were bound to maintain if they became unable to labour. During the year, some coloured citizens of Great Britain, who had been kidnapped and sold into slavery in Cuba, obtained their freedom.—*Class A*, 1842, *pages* 220 *to* 223.—*Class A*, 1843, *pages* 97 *to* 102.

The number of slaves landed in Brazil in 1842 is computed at 14,200, being less than the previous year. Preparations were however making in various parts for carrying on the trade more vigorously. At Macahé, a mercantile house was established with a large capital, for the speedy equipment and fitting out of vessels engaged in the slave trade. The sympathies of the Brazilians being with the slave traders, every aid was given to their vessels to land their cargoes on the coast, and efforts were made to warn them, if a hostile cruizer was known to be approaching. "Fires blazed by night, and signal posts were erected for the express purpose of warning vessels approaching by day, with slaves on board, if a cruizer appeared in the offing."

Of 59 vessels which sailed for Africa this year, from the various ports of Brazil, 24 carried the flag of that country, 13 that of the United States of North America, 11 that of Portugal, 5 that of France, 3 that of Sardinia, 1 that of England, 1 that of Austria, and 1 that of Hamburg. Many of these vessels were ostensibly engaged in lawful commerce. Of the 49 vessels which arrived from Africa during the year, 12 bore the flag of the United States, 12 that of Brazil, 11 that of Portugal, 4 that of France, 2 the Danish, 2 the Austrian, 1 each the Hamburg, English, Sardinian and Swedish. The flags of the other two were not known. These vessels obtained their cargoes generally on the west coast south of the Gulf of Guinea. One only is noted as arriving from the eastern coast.—*Class A*, 1843, *pages* 188, 190, and *Class A*, and *B*, 1842, under head of Rio, Bahia, &c.

Portugal entered into a special treaty with England this year for the suppression of the slave trade.

During the year the direct slave trade was almost suppressed along the coast from Sierra Leone to Gambia. One reason was, the slave factories at Bulama had been destroyed, and the English government had taken possession of the Island under virtue of an agreement made in former times with the native princes. No slaves were known to have been shipped from Pongas or Rio Nunez; yet the trade at Gallinas had partially revived. At Bissao the trade was much checked. Although along this great extent of coast but few slave vessels came for cargoes, yet very many slaves were still carried in the small craft to the Cape Verde's for shipment.

Along the Gulf of Guinea the trade continued, and very many cargoes were shipped from the Islands of St. Thomas and Princes, to which places slaves were gathered from various parts of the neighbouring coasts, particularly from the Gaboon River. South of the equator the trade was prosecuted vigorously, although it had received two important checks, by the destruction of the slave factories at Ambriz and Cabenda.

Little change took place during the year in the slave trade from the eastern coast of Africa, except a small increase of it towards the Persian Gulf. Mehemet Ali, the ruler in Egypt, made protestations against the trade, yet he received slaves in payment of tribute, whom he caused to be sold at public auction in Cairo. At Tripoli and Tunis things remained much as they had been. The Bey of Tunis continued to evince a determination to suppress the trade, and four Circassian females being brought there in an Austrian vessel for sale, he had them set free.—(*See Class D*, 1842, Tunis.)

1843.

In the year 1843, twelve vessels were condemned at Sierra Leone. These had all been engaged in the slave trade to Brazil. Six of them were to obtain cargoes in the Gulf of Guinea, a few degrees north of the equator, five from places south of the equator, and one at Quillimane on the eastern coast. Two only of the twelve had shipped their cargoes when captured.—*Class A*, 1844, *pages* 2, 4. There were on board the two, 837 slaves, of whom 517 were males, and 320 females. There were among the vessels some very small ones, whose accommodations for a living cargo were miserable indeed. The English commissioner in giving his judgment in the case of one of them, the Esperanza, says, "This is by far the most atrocious case presented to this court, since I had the honour of a seat on this bench. Here we find a small vessel, a mere shell, measuring only forty-four tons, ordered to ship about 250 men, women and children. * * * * From the slave deck to the beam, there is only at the highest part thirty-three and a half inches, middle part thirty-one and three-quarter inches; the highest at the wing at midships twenty-three and a half inches, and forward twenty-five inches. Such are the measurements of the height of the hold in which were to be stowed 250 slaves. The very intention of packing 250 fellow creatures in this place of torment and death, is too appalling for contemplation.—*Class A*, 1843, *pages* 46–47. In another of the vessels, the Linda, the space between the slave deck and beam was still more scant, measuring from twenty-two to thirty-inches.—*Class A*, 1844, *page* 16.

At the opening of this year, the slave trade of Cuba was much depressed. The low price which sugar had for some time borne, had discouraged the establishment of new plantations, and had rendered so many of the planters scant of funds, that the market for slaves was any thing but brisk. In addition to this, Captain General Valdez had, by his actions, tended still more to discourage slave traders from landing slaves any where near Havana. The number of those freshly landed seized by his orders, had been a heavy drawback on the profits of the voyages, and this was still more lessened by the increased amount of fees demanded by his subordinates, for screening the balance of the negroes from the arm of the law. Although in many cases thwarted by the officers under him, yet Valdez' energy, together with the depression in the price of sugar, produced such an effect, that during the first part of this year, the people of Havana deemed the trade at an end, and articles intended for the African market, ceased to be in demand. Towards the middle of the year, however, things changed. It was understood that the influences exerted at Madrid, to obtain the recall of Valdez would be successful, and fresh efforts were made to prepare for a revived trade under his successor.—*Class A*, 1844, *pages* 106–113. We have already said, that some of the inhabitants, particularly such planters as had a sufficient stock of slaves, were opposed to the slave trade, and this opposition was much increased by some extensive conspiracies amongst the slaves, discovered this year. A petition was presented to the Governor of Matanzas, remonstrating against the government continuing "to permit the introduction of negroes, to the great injury of the island, and against the wishes of the great majority of the people." The Governor, who derived enormous profits from the slave trade, on reading it, tore it to pieces, and gave the signers to understand, that by that document they laid themselves open to be proceeded against as conspirators. Afterwards, on hearing they intended to present a similar petition to the Captain General of Cuba, he told them if they did not desist, he should be obliged to proceed against them. This did not deter some of them, and several such memorials were laid before Valdez. In short, it appeared to be only the cupidity of the public officers of the Island, and those citizens who were, as capitalists, concerned in the trade, that at this time kept it up in Cuba, few of the inhabitants needing fresh labourers on their estates.

Of the enormous perquisites which the former Captain Generals had derived from the Slave trade, we may form some idea from the following statement. The salary attached to the office, is £3000 per annum, yet the Prince of Anlona, after holding it but twelve months, retired with £30,000 sterling. Espelela, who held it eighteen months, carried home with him £50,000; and Tacon, in three years, realized £80,000. Valdez, who held the office for two years and a half, took with him £1400. One of the Havana tradesmen, speaking of him to the English commissioner, observed, "Oh, he is a fool, he does not know the value of money."—*Class A*, 1843, *p.* 149.

During the year 1843, 347 of the Emancipado negroes were set at liberty, most of them before Valdez was superseded, which occurred in the ninth month. His successor, O'Donnell, reached Havana on the 19th of the tenth month.

The number of slaves introduced into Cuba in 1843, was about 8000, a large increase from 1842, and brought in principally during the latter part of the year. Of the 19 arrivals from Africa, 16 bore the Spanish flag, 2 that of the United States,

1 that of Portugal. Of 23, which cleared out for Africa, 14 carried the Spanish, and 9 the United States flag. A cargo of 900 slaves being brought to Matanzas towards the close of this year, the governor of that place seized the vessel, and before releasing it, made the captain pay much higher fees than had been usually demanded at that port. Thirty thousand dollars were paid to him and his officers, for allowing the landing of this cargo, and besides this, he seized 93 of the newly landed slaves, and declared them to be Emancipados.—*Class A*, 1843, *p.* 148–150.

The number of slaves introduced into Brazil in 1843, is estimated at 30,500. Of 37 cargoes known to have been landed, 3 were obtained from Quillimane on the eastern coast, the rest were from ports in the Gulf of Guinea and south of it, on the western coast; 27 of the cargoes were shipped south of the equator.—*Class A*, 1844, *p.* 183–186.

At Bahia, in Brazil, at and near which many of the slaves were landed, those who had fitted out the vessels which brought them, were generally second class merchants, who combined together and formed joint stock companies, making arrangements with the authorities of the places where they intended to have their cargoes landed. The fees required to give official sanction to this violation of the laws of the country, were paid either in slaves or money. These companies in selecting vessels, generally purchased those built in the United States, as being better sailors, and therefore more likely to escape from the cruizers.

In five of the provinces of Brazil, from the best information which could be obtained by the English resident Consuls, there was a population of three millions, of which one million four hundred thousand were slaves. There was about one million of free coloured people, of which number, however, a few were Indians. The whole number of whites did not much exceed six hundred thousand. The white population, owing to the general laxity of morals among them, increased but slowly, whilst the slaves were receiving a yearly addition from Africa, averaging not much short of 40,000. The increasing preponderance of negro inhabitants, seemed to indicate a fast approaching period, when the slavery of the African race must cease in Brazil. A slight amelioration in the condition of the slaves in that country, was observable in 1843, arising from the increased price the slavers demanded for their new cargoes. It had been a settled principle with some planters there, when slaves were cheap and easily replaced, to work those they had, so constantly during the sugar making season, that human nature sunk under the excess of toil. It was a matter of calculation, how soon the labour of the extra hours they worked a slave, would purchase another to replace him. The effect of the rise in the price of slaves had been, to give an additional value to those held in bondage, and thus to throw a pecuniary shield of defence around them: some planters treating their slaves with compassion and care. On the other hand, Consul Cowper, at Pernambuco, relates some shocking instances of the barbarity of owners. One man, named Antonio Francisco, maimed the slaves who offended him, in the most cruel manner, and had even buried some of them alive. He however met, from private hatred and revenge, the punishment which the magistracy of the country was too weak to inflict. Having caused some of his slaves to murder a political opponent, the neighbouring whites took up arms against him, and he was shot on his own estate. Cowper states, that in this year 1843, whilst he resided in Pernambuco, a public invitation was given by Viora, a man of notorious brutality, to some of his acquaintances, to come to his estate on the following first-day of the week, and see a slave boiled to death. The slave was suspected to have killed his master, and boiling in the large sugar copper of the estate, was the punishment which Viora thought suitable to the supposed offence. Notwithstanding an occasional kind master, Cowper says, the slaves "are kept in a state of the darkest ignorance; they are baptized for form's sake, but are never instructed in relation thereto, and no doubt actually worship the images of the saints, as probably resembling their African gods." *Class B*, 1843, *pages* 363–370.

Soon after Cowper first went to Pernambuco, he, with his

wife, on one occasion, were dining at the table of a fellow countryman, when they heard a noise and disturbance in the entry. This increased—the door was suddenly thrown open, and a black man rushed into the room followed by soldiers. Finding no way of escape, the poor fugitive, for he was a runaway slave, seized a knife from the table and cut his throat from ear to ear, before the company. The soldiers then seized him and dragged him away. The host begged his guests not to be disturbed at the occurrence. Cowper, however, left the table, and followed the poor bleeding body down stairs, and found it on the ground outside of the house. Perceiving the man to be still living, he tied up the wound as well as he could with a handkerchief, and sent for a surgeon. The surgeon did not come for two hours, and when he did, he coolly said it was not worth while to do anything, for the man would not live an hour. Life, however, was not so nearly exhausted in the slave, no large artery had been cut, and he continued to live. On the third day, his master, who had previously refused to do anything for him, had him removed to the hospital. He lived there for three months, and there is little doubt but that if prompt medical attention had been given him, he would have recovered. *Class B*, 1843, *p.* 368.

The ships engaged in the Slave trade from Brazil, the same Consul says, are "daily diminishing the space allowed to these unhappy beings." He mentions one vessel of 21 tons, into which 97 slaves were stowed. Another one, the Temerario, of 381 tons, took on board more than 900 on the African coast. She lost about 100 on the passage, and landed to the great delight of her owners, 816 in Brazil. The rejoicing of the shippers was however soon over,—opthalmia and the small pox were among those landed, and in a few days 300 died. One hundred more never recovered their sight, and were given away to any one who would receive them.

During this year the Slave trade was brisk along the coast of Africa. At Gallinas it was restored, and several cargoes were shipped from thence, and from Bissao, and Rio Pongos. Many were taken from the northern shore of the Gulf of Guinea, but it was south of the equator that the trade was carried on most extensively. Little change had taken place in the eastern Slave trade during the year, although the demand from Muscat was thought to be increasing, as the people were beginning to find it profitable to keep slaves employed in raising sugar cane and manufacturing sugar.

Egypt still continued to send expeditions into the interior of Africa, to destroy villages of nations with which she was not at war, that they might seize the men for her armies, the young girls for her harems, and keep the remainder of the captured for labourers. In the early part of 1843, an expedition of this kind took place, of which we have some of the particulars. It is not often that we have an opportunity of learning the mode of proceeding of those engaged in slave hunts on a large scale. The following authentic account is therefore of much value, showing as it does the enormous expenditure of human life, the grievous amount of human suffering, and the wickedness inseparably connected with such atrocious attempts against the natural rights of mankind. It is a narrative of an expedition of a portion of the Egyptian army, under Ahmed Pasha, undertaken with a view of obtaining slaves. The army intended for this purpose, originally consisted of 2,950 men of the regular infantry, accompanied by 1000 mounted Arabs for cavalry, and had with it four pieces of cannon and 6000 camels. On their march southward, towards the country situated between the White and Blue Nile, they were joined by many Bedouin Arabs, and by an auxiliary force of 600 infantry. The first attack was made on the Denkas negroes, a very numerous people, to some extent agricultural as well as pastoral, who live on the fertile borders of the White Nile, where they find an abundant supply of rich herbage for their cattle, and of grass seeds and wild rice for their own subsistence. It was not deemed necessary that all the troops should be employed in striking this first blow, for as the Denkas were not at war with the Egyptians, it was not supposed that they would be prepared for battle or for offering much resistance to the sudden attack of disciplined and well armed men. To the cavalry and the Bedouins this service was committed, whilst the main body proceeded still further south to Ule. Leopold Weingartshoper, a German physician in the Egyptian service, from whom the incidents of this slave making expedition were derived, being attached to the main body, was not privy to the desolation and horror which these mounted marauders spread through the populous Denka village and neighbourhood which they ravaged. The detachment joined the army five days afterward, bringing with it 623 human captives, 1500 oxen, and a few sheep and goats. The next day the booty was divided, one half being set apart for the government, the other half was divided among the captors.

The army still proceeded southward, and on the 19th of the second month, at Djebel Tombak, in about latitude 10° north, longitude 33° east, a second attack was made on the negroes. In this case the poor blacks had notice of the approach of enemies, and forsaking their village, retired to the summit of a small isolated mountain, near by, for refuge. This spot was surrounded by the Egyptian army, and was soon stormed and carried by it, notwithstanding the desperate defence of the poor negroes, almost every able bodied man of whom was killed or desperately wounded. They had no warlike weapons but bows and arrows with which to repel the invaders, and not one of their assailants lost his life. The conquerors, after securing the prisoners, who, including the infants, were 526 in number, took from the village a portion of the food they found there, and then set fire to the dwellings and consumed them all. The next day, the medical officers of the army, principally Europeans, publicly examined the prisoners, who were found to be a fine large muscular people. There were among them but 75 men at all fit for service, and most of these had severe gun-shot wounds. The Egyptian commander took all these men, and selected the best looking women and children to make up the one-half for the government. From the time of capture up to the period of separation, the prisoners had been quiet, but now, when husbands were torn from their wives, and children, even infants in the arms, from their parents, the cries of distress and anguish were heart rending. The division accomplished, the army proceeded to prepare the prisoners for marching. The neck of each man, and of each able-bodied woman was placed in the crotch of a forked pole, seven or eight feet in length. The two ends of the fork were then securely fastened together behind the prisoner, whose right arm was bound to the pole. This pole was then made fast to the saddle of one of the mounted soldiers, who could thus look after the captives with little trouble to himself. The very old and feeble were led along by ropes tied round their necks. In their journeys the troops were often from six to eight hours without finding water, and the prisoners received none of the supply carried for the use of the soldiers. The sufferings consequent on thirst,—the scanty supply of food allowed them,—and the barbarous manner in which they were hurried along, caused a large mortality among them. Those whose strength failed them, so that they could not keep up with the army, were shot through the head by their cruel drivers, who manifested not the slightest compunction at this wanton destruction of human life. At least one-half of these captives perished before reaching the head quarters, at Khartoom, the junction of the White and Blue Nile.

On the 22d the army proceeded to Kerr, where the inhabitants of a number of small neighbouring villages had taken shelter in two stockades. On the 22d one of these stockades was attacked. Many cannon shots were fired against it, and an opening was at last forced into it by the assailants. The negroes had nothing but their bows and arrows, yet they thrice drove them back from the breach. Fire arms, however, eventually gave the troops the victory. When the enraged soldiery had at last forced themselves inside the stockade, they commenced a scene of butchery. Every one who resisted was shot down, and all whose wounds seemed to unfit them for being slaves. When the bloody work was accomplished, and the prisoners secured, they set fire to the stockade, and leaving the severely wounded, the dying and the dead, to be consumed in the flames, they proceeded to the second place of defence. Ahmed, having had four men severely wounded and 300 slightly so, by the arrows of the negroes, and having had six killed and twelve seriously wounded by musket shots, through the want of skill and discipline among his own soldiers, did not wish to fight any more, but desired rather to make the defenders of the second stockade prisoners by negotiation. He sent one of the captives just taken, with an invitation to them to submit and be slaves. He was unwilling to go on such an errand, saying respecting his countrymen, "I know them well, they will never submit." It proved as he said, they did not deign to answer the summons, and the place was taken by force. Some of the defenders escaped, some were made prisoners, but great numbers were slain. The whole of those captured in the two fortifications, when brought together, proved to be but 463. About 500 oxen and a few sheep were all the additional booty driven off; the numerous swine being left behind, no Moslem being willing to touch one of them.

The government half of these slaves were sent under escort to Khartoom, but many of the soldiers sold theirs at very low prices to the Arabian traders, who accompanied the army. Boys of ten or twelve years of age, sold at seven Turkish piasters, something less than one shilling and six pence sterling; and one old woman brought but seven pence half penny.

At Kirmuk, a large village of Boran negroes, the army arrived on the 1st of the third month. The place containing, it was thought, 1600 huts, had been deserted of all its inhabitants, who had fled to the summit of a mountain. The village was burnt by the Egyptian army, and on the morning of the 3rd, a large force proceeded to attack the negroes in their place of defence, whilst the cavalry and mounted Bedouins kept watch on every side, to seize all who might attempt to escape. The first battalion of infantry in ascending the mountain, came on an inclosure containing about 1200 women and children. Desirous of booty, the men stopped and commenced binding and carrying them away. Whilst thus engaged, the Boran men who had been watching them from above, suddenly descended and fell on them with loud cries. This unlooked for attack, produced a panic, their slaves and loaded muskets were dropped, and the whole battalion fled down the mountain precipitately. In their descent the fugitives encountered three other battalions, with the company of auxiliary troops coming up, and as they rushed furiously through the advancing company, they infected all with a like panic. The whole body retreated in confusion. The loss of a number of both officers and men, and perhaps more than all, of some hundred muskets, prepared the Egyptian leader to listen to the terms offered him by the Borans, who promised to pay a tribute of fifteen ounces of gold, if he would retire. This he gladly did.

From one other village, the army obtained a few captives. On the return of the expedition, it fell into the route of the escort, who had started to take to Khartoom the slaves made at Kerr. It was appalling to find so many dead bodies marking the path pursued by the company. The whole number of negroes captured in this expedition, was 1875; but another branch of the Egyptian army, which had gone at the same time negro hunting into Nubia, returned to Khartoom with more than 5000.—*Class D,* 1843, *pages* 166–169.

1844.

During the year 1844 the slave trade appears to have been prosecuted with the same unblushing effrontery and determination as heretofore, though perhaps not with the same success. The whole number of slaves computed to have been exported westward from Africa in this year, (according to the report of the select committee on the slave trade, appointed by the House of Commons,) was 54,102, of which number 13,525 are supposed to have perished during the voyage.* Forty-nine of the vessels engaged in the trade were captured, twelve of which had slaves on board, and the remaining thirty-seven were fitted for the traffic, but were taken before having the opportunity for shipping their wretched cargoes. On board the twelve vessels captured after loading, were found 3,519 slaves. The tonnage of all these twelve vessels is not given, but from what is specified, some idea may be formed of the dreadful manner in which the innocent victims of a brutalizing cupidity were crowded into

* 4th Report to H. C. p. 3.

them. Thus, one of ninety-nine tons had 70; one of little more than thirty-five tons had 282; one of eighty-five tons had 336; one of near ninety-five tons had 421; one of nearly sixty-seven tons had 431; and another of little more than eighty-one tons had 312 slaves on board; showing an average of five persons for each ton, besides the crew and necessary stores. The vessels captured carrying the Spanish flag, had obtained their cargoes at the Sherbro, at Ambriz, Cabinda or Loanda, and were generally bound for the Island of Cuba, while those sailing under the flag of Brazil had loaded some where in the Bight of Benin, or on the coast of Benguela, and were bearing away for Rio, Pernambuco, Bahia, Mecahé, or San Francisco de Sal.

The vessels which succeeded in escaping the vigilance of the cruizers, and crossed the Atlantic, are believed to have landed 10,000 captives in the Spanish colony, and 26,000 in Brazil. —P. 4th "Rep." to H. C. p. 3.

The Portuguese Government at home appeared desirous to fulfil the stipulations of the treaty of 1842, and few vessels of that nation were found openly engaged in the illicit traffic; but the officers in her dominions on the African coast, as we have before observed, were generally either engaged in the trade themselves, or disposed to connive at its prosecution, for the sake of the gold, with which many of them were openly bribed. At the Cape de Verdes they continued to furnish passports to vessels engaged in the traffic, and the British Commissioners in their report, dated Boa-vista, December 1st, 1844, say, that no person acquainted with the appearance of newly made slaves, can walk the streets of that town, without being aware that they are introduced there, and it was well known they were shipped from thence, and from other of the islands across the Atlantic.

The Commissioners at the Cape of Good Hope, represent the trade as being carried on to a considerable extent, from the Portuguese possessions in the Mozambique, from whence the slaves were shipped to Brazil. Prior to 1844, Great Britain had concluded eleven treaties with various of the native chiefs of Africa, for the suppression of the slave trade; and in this year another was added thereto. Notwithstanding the temptations held out to them, there can be no doubt that the terms of these treaties were generally observed by those contracting them, and they ceased from dealing in their fellow countrymen; but yet the Commissioners at Sierre Leone, who have ample opportunity for acquiring a correct knowledge of the trade in its several departments say, "we believe that the slave trade is increasing, and that it is conducted perhaps more systematically than it has ever been before. The actual exports of negroes from all points of the coast, appear to be now *chiefly* carried on under the flags of Brazil and Spain; there can be no question however, that indirectly the flags of other nations continue to be used in aid of the traffic."

Notwithstanding the professions of the government of Brazil, and the provisions of the treaty of 1826, which declare it piracy to engage in the slave trade, yet it continued to be openly carried on in nearly all the ports of her extended coast, and the functionaries, from the highest to the lowest, with but few exceptions, still receive a large pecuniary emolument from the traffic. The British Commissioners in their Report for this year say;—

"Every exertion has been made to render this return [return of slaves landed in Rio in 1844,] correct, but notwithstanding, we have good reason to believe, that many vessels have landed their cargoes of human beings, of which no notice has reached us. This part of the Brazilian coast affords such vast facilities for this description of contraband, and the establishments at the numerous and well adapted landing places are now so efficiently prepared and managed, and so securely protected by the surrounding authorities, that the rapidity, security and secresy with which 500 or 600 slaves are taken from a vessel, and she in a few hours after, anchored in the harbour of this capital, is surprising. The proprietors in the localities, the best adapted for these clandestine proceedings, such as the neighbourhood of Campos, Cape Frio, Ilka Grande, and Santos, are reaping a rich harvest, and even the appointment to the municipal offices in those districts, is said to be now an object of eager competition."—*Class A*, 1845, *page* 507.

Of the manner in which this illicit trade was prosecuted, we obtain the following information from one of the Consuls at Pernambuco; his letter is dated May 16th, 1845.

"The mode in which the African Slave Trade was formerly conducted in this port, has now assumed a new feature. Instead of the larger classes of vessels, varying from 150 to 300 tons burthen each, a smaller kind is now employed, of from 45 to 60 tons, namely, "Maria," 52 tons admeasurement, "Maraquinhas," 52, "Deliberecio," 54, two "Delegencies," of 54 and 55, and the "San Domingos," of 56 tons burden. These insignificant looking craft, rigged with boom, main and fore-sails only, sail fast, are of light draught of water, and low built, that they may more easily escape detection; their complement of crew varies from eight to fourteen men, who are engaged by the run, and whose interests being solely contingent on the voyage being prosperous, are always on the alert. These vessels, as their predecessors did, take on board their cargoes of small packages of cotton goods, (packed expressly for this traffic,) are despatched for Aracaty, Ceara, or some other of the northern parts of this empire, as a blind. . . . When free from observation, they stretch across the Atlantic for the effectuation of their nefarious voyage. . . When approaching the African coast, the crew keep a vigilant watch, and seizing the first favourable moment, dash into some of the small creeks, where concealed by the mangrove bushes, they instantly land their cargoes; the packages being all small, capable of being conveyed to the shore on a man's head, facilitates the discharge; and should the unfortunate victims of the owner's cupidity be collected in sufficient numbers to fill the vessel, they are as speedily transferred from the shore to the miserable den, sufficiently noxious when only a moderate number, (as the slave merchants call 100,) but when from 150 to 300 beings are stowed in the hold of one of these small craft, without space to lay down, nay, scarcely to stir, the stench and filth must be execrable: humanity shudders at such a picture of misery. It is certain, that if the vessel is secure from pursuit or danger, the captain will, from motives of interest, not of benevolence, allow his wretched captives to breathe a pure air, by admitting alternate portions to enjoy a temporary refreshment on deck. On nearing the Brazil coast, more attention is requisite, and a good watch is kept for any cruizers. If all is clear, the vessel proceeds to the preconcerted place of disembarkation." * * Una is a favourite spot, and Catuama is another refuge for this illicit traffic. At the former, all is safe. The Vicar of that small town superintends the landing of the slaves, receiving for such service twenty-one shillings and three pence sterling, for every slave landed alive."—*Class B*, 1845, *p.* 443.

One of the Portuguese vessels captured this year, had shipped her slaves at Cape Lopez, and was on her way to the Island of St. Thomas, but it would appear that very few slaves were introduced into the Portuguese West India possessions.

The Cuban Slave Trade, which under the vigorous administration of General Valdez had been almost annihilated, revived immediately on his being recalled home; and being protected and encouraged by his successor, Leopold O'Donnell, it had rapidly increased. The Commissioners stationed in Havana, by the British Government, in reporting to the Earl of Aberdeen, state, that twenty-one vessels landed cargoes of slaves in the island; and the "list gives in round numbers a total of 7280 (slaves,) of cargoes actually known, together with three other arrivals, of which the number were not given, and a remaining conviction, that several vessels have come to other parts of the island, of which the particulars could not be ascertained. Adding therefore one-third to our number, as heretofore, on these accounts, I have, (he says,) with much regret, to express an opinion, that about 10,000 unhappy beings have been brought here into slavery during the past year." Of the eighteen vessels that left Havana suspected of being engaged in the slave trade, six were American.—*Class A*, 1845, *p.* 378.

During this year an insurrection was supposed to have been planned among the slaves in this island, extensive in its ramifications and contemplating the entire destruction of the cruel oppressors of the blacks. How far the fears of the merciless masters exaggerated the dangers to which they supposed themselves to be exposed, by the machinations of those whom by their cruelty they were goading on to seek redress and revenge, it is impossible now to ascertain; but it is certain that the occasion was made use of to inflict the most inhuman cruelties upon the poor blacks on the island, both bond and free. In the Report of a subsequent year, the Consul General says:

"For obvious reasons, the great destruction of human life by the cruelties inflicted on the slaves during the terrific persecution of 1844, has been concealed as much as possible; but the poor wretches were sacrificed in every possible way, crowded into the most loathsome prisons and other places of confinement, left to die in the stocks, and of the wounds inflicted upon them by direction of merciless fiscals, and the application of the lash, under which numbers expired, from whom no sort of confession could be extorted. Whether they were guilty, or had even been accused, they were treated just the same; vast numbers were thus destroyed in every district of the island, besides those that were executed publicly, under sentence of the military commissions." It was supposed that about 1000 free blacks were expelled from the island that year, by the Governor General. These being mostly artizans, possessing some education and property, were deemed dangerous.—*Class B*, 1848, *page* 42.

But although heretofore Spain, Portugal and Brazil have appeared to be most deeply implicated in the illicit Slave trade, the latter, as the largest slave importing country in the world, being preeminent in the guilt attached to it, yet numerous facts were occurring in every year, and noticed in the Reports of the officers of the British naval force on the coast of Africa, showing how fully American citizens were connected with the traffic, and prostituting the flag of their country for the purpose of sharing its profits and screening those who were carrying it on. In 1843, the American Consul, at Rio de Janeiro, wrote to the Secretary of State upon the subject, showing the manner in which our citizens were aiding and abetting the Slave trade; but it was not until the present year (1844) that the correspondence of the United States Minister at the court of Brazil, fully developed the manner in which a large and important part of the nefarious transactions connected with this trade, was conducted by our countrymen.

The following extracts from a communication from Henry A. Wise, the American Minister at Rio, to Maxwell, Wright & Co., commission merchants of that city, who had applied to him for information regarding the legality of disposing of American vessels at that port, deliverable on the coast of Africa or elsewhere; or of taking charters to carry cargoes to the same coast, will serve to show the nature, connections, and extent of the African Slave trade, as carried on by citizens of the United States, under the protection of its flag.

"It cannot be denied, and it is no longer to be concealed (and the sooner all parties, at home and abroad are informed of it, the better,) that *there is no trade whatever*, between the coast of Africa and Brazil, but what partakes directly or indirectly of the nature, and of the profits or losses, of the Slave trade. The Slave trade is the main, the staple business, and all other trades, with the slightest exception, are accessory or auxiliary to it, between that coast (particularly the parts about Congo and Cabinda) and Brazil. And no vessels of the United States are chartered for the coast, in this country, but to export goods, provisions, and munitions of war, to make funds for the Slave trade; or they are chartered to carry and bring crews of vessels employed in the Slave trade, and to be tenders of those vessels in other respects; or they are chartered to cover their sales, and to obtain the protection of their flag, until they can be delivered on the coast, and ship their cargo of slaves. And they are chartered by and sold to none, or scarcely ever to any one, except notorious slave dealers, and are consigned in almost every instance, to their known agents in Africa. And extraordinary prices are given for the vessels and the charters of vessels of the United States, because their national flag alone protects them from visits and search. And all this is so notorious here, and the ways and means of doing this are so well known here—the charter parties being almost stereotyped—that there is not an intelligent, observing or enquiring citizen of the United States in Rio de Janeiro, who has resided here three months, but what may be said to know, and could, with the legal means, easily verify the objects, purposes, and intents, for which such charters and sales of vessels, deliverable on the coast of Africa, are made. And the general knowledge and the general intent could, in almost every instance be proved, if there was full power to compel the attendance of witnesses, and to make them answer under oath. A vessel is apparently chartered by the month, at so much per month for the coast to cover her on the voyage to Africa with the United States flag. The charter party binds her to take *over passengers*—meaning a Brazilian or Portuguese master and crew, who are in fact to navigate her back with a cargo of slaves, without either flag, or papers, or nationality, running all risks of capture. But she has, in fact, been actually sold, deliverable on the coast, the whole or greater part of her purchase money has been advanced here as security for the sale; her charter and sale have been negotiated by an English broker, directly with the slave dealer, and he gets two and a half per cent. commission. The advance of the purchase money here as security, and the guarantee of the payment of the whole charter and sale, is made; and two and a half per cent. commission is charged for that, besides two and a half per cent. for doing the business, and two and a half per cent. more for remittance to the United States, making ten per cent. at least, on the whole transaction of charter and sale. The master of the vessel is ordered and authorized to take on the coast, in case it be offered, the sum already bargained and guaranteed to be given here, and the agent of the slave trading purchaser in Africa, is written to, and ordered by him to offer and give the same sum already agreed upon, and partly paid here. The vessel is loaded with English goods "fit for the coast," that is, with goods which are the medium of exchange there, fit for slaves (money not being used or known there) and with Brazilian provisions of jerked beef, black beans, farina, and cacheca, and sometimes with bar and hoop iron, and with powder and muskets; and there is another vessel chartered in like manner already there, or going, or gone, or soon to go, with a like cargo, to make Slave trade funds, and to supply the Slave trade employees, and according to her charter party, and a private understanding with the first vessel, to bring back as "*passengers*" the American crew of the first vessel, at the cost of the charterer; and the first is sold and delivered; and her American master and crew have very *particular written* instructions by some business friend here, how far to go, exactly, in order to avoid the laws of the United States—to take off the flag, the name on the stern, and the vessel's papers, and to exercise no act of ownership, and to give no aid or assistance after sale and delivery, and neither before nor after to aid or abet the Slave trade in any way. And in most cases these instructions are very scrupulously followed; and in from two to seven hours after the vessel is sold and delivered, she is loaded to suffocation, with hundreds of miserable captives, already on the beach in shackles; who are berthed on water-pipes, laid level fore and aft, covered with rush mats; and instantly she sails for the first port she can reach in safety, on the coast of Brazil; and her American master and crew are transported to the second vessel, which, during the time of her waiting, is employed, perhaps, in transporting and carrying supplies along the coast, from slave factory to slave factory—from Cabinda to Congo, and from Congo to Cabinda, and which, as soon as she gets her returning "*passengers,*" who have carried a vessel over directly to the slavers, and carried the *slavers* themselves over, returns, perhaps, with a lawful cargo of wax, ivory, &c., which has been brought from the interior to the coast of Africa, on the heads of the very captives which her consort has just sailed with to the first port in Brazil." * * *

"I know that these acts have heretofore been considered perfectly lawful. * * * * * I had no conception of the extent, the universality, and the notoriety of the traffic, until duly called upon to aid in arresting its crimes. To my utter astonishment, I found nothing but error of opinion, both as to morals and legal obligations upon the whole subject, even amongst the best informed and most respectable American citizens. It is needless to inquire how this state of things came to exist. In the first place, the habitudes of thought and action among our citizens in Brazil, in respect to this trade, have been forming for a long time, and, I must add, that they have grown and strengthened by long *neglect* on the part of our government, and its proper authorities, whose duty it was to enlighten and instruct our business men, and to prevent errors and misconceptions, and offences on the part of every body. The apathy at home on this subject is attributed, justly, to an almost total ignorance of its importance and consequences, and especially of its details. * * * * In the second place, the silence of the State Department, and the professional and official opinions that have been given, that I have seen, on the subject embraced in your note to me, have been, it so happened, though sound in their law as far as they go, *of a tendency rather* to confirm than to correct errors, because they did not go far enough to meet the cases as they actually arise here. * * * On the 5th of October, 1843, Mr. Slacum wrote to Mr. Upshur, No. 71, in relation to the case of the 'Parmelia,' showing the almost direct manner in which our citizens are 'aiding and abetting the Slave trade, &c.,' in relation to the brig 'Yankee,' which landed a cargo of nearly 700 slaves; and in relation to the vessel 'Sterling.' In this letter he says,—'To the enquiry, why American vessels are preferred and sought after by the slave dealers, and why they are willing to pay such high prices for them? it may be answered, that no other flag carries with it the same immunities. The flag of the Powers, parties to the quintuple treaty, affords no protection against detention, search, and capture. So with Brazil and Portugal. Hence the Slave dealer looks to our commercial marine, to enable him to carry on the trade—I mean so far as regards the transportation hence to Africa, of the necessary *equipments, provisions, water* and *vessels*. Having once got these indispensable adjuncts to the traffic to the coast, half the risk is over. He must then take his chance for the other half, that is the return voyage—and in which he is very often successful. * * * * A vessel is *chartered or secretly sold* to a slave dealer, to be delivered on the coast. She carries a cargo, and in some instances the very persons, *as passengers,* who are to navigate her back,—all the slave dealer requires. She is overhauled and examined by an American man-of-war. Every thing appears to be in due form. The cargo, be it what it may, (except slaves, as I understand) affords no just ground of capture. She passes on, delivers her freight, and returns for another cargo; or is then transferred to new masters, takes in slaves, waits for a propitious moment, makes her escape from the coast under any and all flags, with other papers and a new crew, and runs the hazard for her destined port. It is not long since, that an American vessel sailed hence for the coast, having part of her cargo cleared and shipped as *wine*; but on her arrival there, it turned out to be ninety pipes of fresh water! a much more valuable article than wine. This vessel was the brig 'Duan,' of Beverly, Massachusetts, Capt. Ezra Foster, &c. The truth is, all these vessels are either owned by, or are in the service of slave dealers; and the trade will continue, until some other measures are adopted by our government to put an end to it." * * * * * *

"For reasons entirely unconnected with this subject, and without imputation, either on his official or personal conduct, I believe Mr. Slacum was removed from his office, and left it on or about April, 1844. The Slave Trade has been continued and been increasing between Brazil and Africa ever since. It was literally continued; for the very vessel the "*Montevideo*," which his last letter on the subject of the trade notified the department of, is the vessel, the master and crew of which are now here prisoners. The other cases are numerous. The "*Ganneclift*" has also since landed a cargo of slaves, the "*Sooy*," of Newport, Rhode Island, landed another cargo, and was run ashore in chase, by a British man-of-war: the "*Agnes*," whose voyage had its "incipiency" in the United States, has landed lately two cargoes of slaves; and the "Sea Eagle," of Boston, the tender of the "*Agnes*" and "*Montevideo*," has just sailed on another charter-party to Africa, with "*passengers;*" the brig "*Susan and Mary*," or "Susan Mary" (American,) having sailed on the 21st ultimo for Angola, with passengers.—
* * * * *

"The ship-owners at home, in many cases I hope, ignorant of what enhances the ships here, write peremptory orders to the consignees in Brazil, to negotiate charter-parties on sales of their vessels. One chief consideration of sending vessels here with cargoes, is to sell the ships; and both are consigned to those who will negotiate charters and sales to the best advantage. If the commission merchants here refuse to obey orders, they necessarily lose their best customers, and the most profitable part of their business. If they do not touch these negotiations, they will, in fact, be stopped also of their regular and lawful chance of gain. Let the whole country then, at home, be fully informed of the *reason* why vessels are chartered and sold here at extraordinary high prices; that the African Slave Trade alone can afford to pay such high prices; that that trade alone does pay them; and that charters and sales here are, in one word, charters and sales to that trade, and that to sell vessels deliverable on the coast, chartered to take *passengers* over, is here notoriously nothing less than to sail a vessel and crew over to Africa, under the protection of the United States flag, with the intent to deliver it for the purposes, and to aid and abet the Slave Trade. Let this be known, and then let us see, what respectable owners of vessels and cargoes, whose custom is worth having, will make consignees here pay penalty for refusing to aid and abet the Slave Trade."—*Class D,* 1845, *p.* 118–124.

The following extract from a letter addressed by the same individual, to Hâmilton Hamilton, the British Minister, at the Brazilian coast, is further illustrative of the manner in which the trade is conducted. It is dated, December 1st, 1844.

"It is said, and I am convinced truly, that the trade to and from Africa and Brazil, particularly that part of the coast of the former, in and about Cabinda and Congo, with very little exception, is the buying and selling, and transportation of slaves; and that the entire trade, with very little exception, in dry goods, provisions, crockery, cacheca, muskets, powder, iron, and all other articles, but contributes, and is only auxiliary to, the one great business of capturing and enslaving the negroes;

this is too notorious to be denied in Rio de Janeiro. The passengers from Brazil, to carry whom is almost always a stipulation of the charter parties of our vessels, are mostly masters and crews of Brazil, taken hence to bring the slave vessels and their cargoes back; and those brought back from Africa by our vessels, are mostly American masters and crews, who have carried our vessels out. Those passengers who are not either masters, mates, or of the crews of Brazil or the United States, are either agents or owners of vessels, or are factors, agents, or employés, in some capacity or other, of the large rich slave dealers; or are merchants, or their factors and agents, who are going and coming to look after the proceeds of their goods, shipped at immense profit, to make funds for the one great trade in the staple article of slaves.

"No such thing as money proper, or cash, is known scarcely among the African tribes, on that part of the coast, of which I am speaking. They buy and sell by the measure of cotton, cloth, or of aguardiènte. The only medium of exchange among the Africans is in the form of goods, wares, and merchandize, by barter; and that between the agents there and the large slave dealers, or in goods for that market in this country, is in the form of bills, on Brazil. The very ivory and other products of Africa for export, are brought from the interior to the coast, on the heads of the negroes, who are themselves to be shipped as slaves."

"It is said that there is not a merchant or dealer of any sort on this whole coast, from Para to Rio Grande, engaged in the trade between Brazil and Africa, who does not, directly or indirectly participate in the profit or loss of the foreign Slave Trade. And there is very little loss in that trade. Nothing is lost if two out of five trips succeed, and that trade has of late rather increased than diminished. It has decreased perhaps to Rio de Janeiro, but increased to every other province of Brazil. By the estimation of very good authority I am informed, that there will probably have been imported into Brazil not less than 30,000 slaves, the present year of 1844. Since my arrival in this city on the 2nd of August last, I can specify the vessels that have brought about 3,000 to this coast, between Cape Frio and Victoria." * * * * * * "Slave decks are no longer used, the water casks stowed level in one or more tiers, according to the size of the vessel, fore and aft, and rush mats spread over them, is the last improvement of fitting a slaver; and they can now ship—indeed, it is proved under oath in this examination, that it took the 'Montevideo,' with a swept hold, from but two to seven hours, to ship a cargo of 800 slaves; they have their water pipes filled, and buried in the sand of the beach, and the slaves, the farina, the jerked beef, the provisions and stores, and the water, are moved at a moment's warning in canoes and launches, to the vessel waiting at the distance of five minutes row from the shore."—*Class B*, 1845, *page* 253.

In order that his government at home should be put in possession of a knowledge of the manner in which its citizens were transgressing its laws, and bringing disgrace on its national character, the Minister transmitted copies of the communications from which the foregoing extracts are taken, to J. C. Calhoun, then Secretary of State, and from his official correspondence with the Secretary, we take the following:

"These papers but too clearly show how the African Slave trade is carried on in Brazil, and how shamefully the United States flag is prostituted to its infamous uses. Our laws should be modified to meet this way of aiding and abetting the Slave trade, by the sale of vessels here, to be transferred and delivered on the coast of Africa. Thus it is that our flag is made to protect a Brazilian vessel, with a crew, and perfect outfit of slave-deck, water casks, irons, &c., to the African coast; and I venture to affirm, that not a vessel of the United States is sold in Brazil, to be delivered at a port in Africa, without taking out a crew and such outfit for the Slave trade, and without the United States captain and crew, if not owners and consignees, wilfully and knowingly aiding and abetting that traffic; and I affirm further, that in all cases the United States Consul has reason to know, and does know to a moral certainty, that in every such case without exception, there is more or less preparation for, and an intention to engage in the Slave trade, if opportunity favours the attempt, when any such vessel clears from his office in Brazil."—*Class D*, 1845, *p*. 91.

Rio de Janeiro, Dec. 14, 1844.

"The accompanying papers * * * will show the nature, connections and extent of the African Slave trade, as it is, and has for some time, been unblushingly carried on by our citizens under our flag. It has grown so bold and so bad as no longer to wear a mask, even to those who reside here, and who are all acquainted with the trade between Brazil and Africa, * * I must say it [an official examination] has developed a combination of persons and means to carry on this infamous traffic, to the utter disgrace of human nature, and to the dishonour of our flag, and of all three nations—England, Brazil and the United States. I have carefully abstained from mentioning names, but I earnestly submit to the Department, that the attention of Congress ought at once to be called to the amendment of our laws for the suppression of the African Slave trade, and to the crying injustice of punishing the poor ignorant officers and crews of merchant ships, for high misdemeanors and felonies, when the ship-owners in the United States, and their American consignees, factors, and agents abroad, are left almost untouched by penalties, for sending the sailors on voyages, notoriously for the purposes of the Slave trade."—*Class D*, 1845, *p*. 103.

The President of the United States, transmitted to Congress copies of the despatches received from the Minister at Rio, upon the subject of the Slave trade, with a special message, in which he says, "it cannot but be a subject of the most profound regret, that any portion of our citizens should be found acting in co-operation with the subjects of other powers, in opposition to the policy of their government; thereby subjecting to suspicion, and to the hazard of disgrace, the flag of their own country. It is true that this traffic is carried on altogether in foreign ports, and that our own coasts are free from its pollution, but the crime remains the same, wherever perpetrated, and there are many circumstances to warrant the belief, that some of our citizens are deeply involved in its guilt."

The mode of proceeding in the Slave trade, as detailed by the United States Minister, had claimed the attention of the officers of the British government employed in Brazil, and on the coast of Africa, and it is thus noticed in one of the Reports already alluded to.

" The most successful adventures to the coast of Africa, during 1844, were those accomplished with the assistance of vessels under the American flag. The plan has been to employ two vessels under charters, sending them to Africa from this place with cargoes adapted for African marts, and also with water and other equipments for the transport of slaves. One of these vessels proceeds to trade at the different African ports, under the direction of the chief supercargo, while the other remains stationary, as a store ship, at the place where the negroes are collected for embarkation. This stationary vessel, generally one which has, according to the terms of a former charter, been two or three previous voyages, is then, under the conditions frequently found in such contracts, delivered over to the charterers as their property; when being prepared for the reception of the slaves, and all the time under an illegal flag, she is crammed with slaves as soon as the opportunity offers, and proceeds to her private rendezvous in Brazil. Thither also her consort returns in ballast with part of the crew of the other vessel on board, and in all probability assists, should occasion require, to decoy the cruizers from the vessel taking the slaves. This outrageous prostitution of the flag of the United States, was instanced in our last Report. The great profit which this arrangement left to the parties, having increased of late the employment of American vessels, the authorities of the United States have been vigilantly exerting themselves, and have lately added much to the former legal evidence they had collected of these criminal transactions on the part of American citizens. Several individuals implicated, are in consequence now under American custody here, and others are on their way to the United States for trial."—*Class A*, 1845, *p.* 508.

The Earl of Aberdeen, in a communication to the American Minister, at London, calls his attention to the subject, and gives the names of the American Brig "Yankee," the "Leda," the "Sophia" and the "Illinois," as having been detected in these nefarious transactions.

That the cruelty, the indifference to human suffering, and the disregard of human life which characterize the slave trade, are equally manifested on board vessels which have been carrying the American flag, as those of any another nation, is shown by the following extract, from a deposition made before the American Consul at Rio, by one of the crew of the "Kentucky," an American vessel, navigated to the east coast by an American master and crew. The "Kentucky" had taken in her cargo of 500 slaves at Inhambane. "And deponent further saith, that the next day after the vessel crossed the bar on leaving Inhambane as aforesaid, the negroes rose upon the officers and crew; a majority of the men, all of whom were in irons, got their irons off, broke through the bulk-head into the females department, and likewise into the forecastle. Upon this, the captain armed the crew with cutlasses, and got all the muskets and pistols and loaded them, and the crew were firing down among the slaves for half an hour or more. In about half an hour they were subdued and became quiet again. The slaves were then brought on deck, eight or ten at a time, and ironed afresh. They were re-ironed that afternoon and put below, except about seven, who remained on deck. None were killed on this occasion, and but eight or ten wounded. They fired with balls in the pistols, and shot in the muskets. Supposes the reason none were killed, is that they had to fire through the grates of the hatches, and the slaves got out of the way as much as they could. On the next day they were brought upon deck, two or three dozen at a time, all being well ironed; and tried by Captain Fonseca and officers, and within two or three days afterward, forty-six men and one woman were hung and shot, and thrown overboard. They were ironed or chained, two together, and when they were hung, a rope was put round their necks, and they drawn up to the yard arm, clear of the sail. This did not kill them, but only choked or strangled them. They were then shot in the breast and the bodies thrown overboard. If only one, of two that were ironed together, was to be hung, a rope was put round his neck, and he was drawn up clear of the deck, and his leg laid across the rail and chopped off, to save the irons and release him from his companion, who at the same time lifted up his leg 'till the other was chopped off as aforesaid, and he released. The bleeding negro was then drawn up, shot in the breast, and thrown overboard, as aforesaid. The legs of about one dozen were chopped off in this way. When the feet fell on deck, they were picked up by the Brazilian crew and thrown overboard, and sometimes at the body, while it still hung living, and all kinds of sport were made of the business. When two that were chained together were both to be hung, they were hung together by their necks, shot, and thrown overboard, irons and all. When the woman was hung up and shot, the ball did not take effect, and she was thrown overboard living, and was seen to struggle some time in the water before she sunk; and deponent further said, that after this was over, they brought up and flogged about twenty men and six women. When they were flogged they were laid flat on the deck, and their hands tied and secured to one ring bolt, and their feet to another. They were then whipped by two men at a time, by one with a stick about two feet long, with five or six strands of raw hide secured to the end of it; and by the other with a piece of the hide of a sea-horse; this was a strip about four feet long, from half an inch to an inch wide, as thick as one's finger and thicker, and hard as whalebone, but more flexible. The flogging was very severe. * * * All the women that were flogged at this time died, but none of the men; many of them however were sick all the passage, and were obliged to lie on their bellies during the remainder of the voyage, and some of them could hardly get on shore on arrival at Cape Frio. The flesh of some of them where they were flogged, putrified, and came off in some cases six or eight inches in diameter, and in places half an inch thick. Their wounds were dressed and filled up by the Contre Mestre, with farina and cacheca, made into poultice, and sometimes with a salve made on board. When the farina and cacheca were applied to the poor creatures, they would shiver and tremble for half an hour, and groan and sob with the most intense agony. They were a shocking and horrible sight during the whole passage." *Class A*, 1845, *page* 518.

We have dwelt longer upon the participation of American citizens in this nefarious traffic, as exhibited in 1844, because of it being the first year in which the manner and extent of this participation was developed, by one holding a high official station under the government of the United States, and who, while residing at the greatest slave mart in Brazil, had ample opportunity of making himself acquainted with the shifts resorted to, and the crimes committed by his countrymen, while participating in the profits arising from a trade denounced by their government as piracy and as deserving of the severest punishment. We shall find, however, that notwithstanding these facts were published for the information of the public, and the attention of Congress was called to the subject, no more efficient measures for preventing the extension of the essential aid to Slave dealers, that has so long been afforded by American citizens, have been taken, and the annual Reports upon the Slave trade, are constantly giving undeniable evidence that American vessels, commanded and manned by our citizens, and with the connivance of their owners, continue to embark in this illicit commerce, and to prostitute and disgrace the flag of their country, by using it to cover and carry out the schemes of those abandoned men, who, for the love of gold, are willing to incur the guilt of buying and selling their fellow men.

Of the efforts for the suppression of the trade made in 1844, we may notice, that Spain enacted more stringent penal laws against the prosecution of the Slave trade, attaching various penalties of imprisonment, fine and banishment to their infringement. In a treaty of Amity, Commerce, and Navigation, between Venezuela and New Granada, ratified in this year, they mutually agree to preserve in force, the laws relative to the abolition of the Slave trade, and to adopt every measure that appeared necessary for preventing any citizen of either State, from taking part in such traffic; and the government of Bolivia enacted a law by which any one, native or foreigner, who, under the national flag should trade in slaves, or introduce them into Bolivia, either by land or sea, should be accounted guilty of piracy, and suffer ten years imprisonment.

1845.

Notwithstanding the apparent intention of Spain to comply with her engagements, and restrain her subjects from continuing in the trade—and although Portugal said she had strictly forbid the governors of her African dominions from conniving at it, yet its diminution in 1845 was comparatively small. The enormous profits realized by the Slave traders, notwithstanding the loss sustained by the capture of a large number of their vessels and the perfection to which their organization had been brought, proved sufficient to animate them with confidence in the final success of their adventures, and allowed the trade to flag but little, either in extent or activity.

The number of slaves taken from Africa in this year, to supply the markets of the western world, appears not to have been less than 36,758, being a falling off from the number of the preceding year of 17,344. Of this 36,758, twenty-five per cent. or 9,189, are supposed to have perished on the middle passage; and 3,519 were captured by the cruizers of different nations.* Eighty-seven vessels engaged in the trade were captured by the British naval force, the tonnage of which range from twenty-eight to 417 tons, the most of them being between 130 and 220 tons burden. Of the eighty-seven captured, eleven had slaves on board. The greatest number of those detected in the trade, were sailing under the Brazilian flag; and those with this flag which were loaded with slaves, averaged $6\frac{1}{10}$ persons to each ton. Vessels carrying the Spanish flag were the next in number, and averaged $4\frac{1}{5}$ to the ton, while those sailing without any flag, of which there were a considerable number, averaged nearly four. Some vessels under the flags of Portugal, of France,† of Buenos Ayres, and several with the flag of the United States, were found participating in the trade. Some

---

* 4th Report to H. C., p. 3. † Report to H. L., Appendix, pages 359 and 363.

idea of the great extent of the Brazilian Slave trade in this year, may be formed from the fact, that of the eighty-seven vessels captured by the naval force of Great Britain, for being engaged in the trade, sixty-one were Brazilian, and it is probable that some of those taken by the French and Portuguese were of the same national character. Of the slaves exported from Africa westward, 22,700 were landed in the different parts of Brazil.

It is impossible to ascertain, by the registers kept at the Custom houses in the different ports of Brazil, the number of vessels arriving from Africa, inasmuch as the practice constantly obtains, of vessels returning from Africa running into outports on the coast, and landing their cargoes there; large store houses, and other establishments necessary for the outfit of slaves being openly kept at those places by the Slave dealers. Thus, in 1845, the departures from Rio de Janeiro for Africa, exceeded the arrivals from that country by 32, there being 55 of the former, and 23 of the latter. Of the departures, 14 sailed under the flag of the United States, and of the arrivals, there were eight of the same nation. In addition to the uncertainty arising from this cause, it is notorious, that the government officers connive at the practice of issuing false clearances. In consequence of these difficulties in ascertaining the operations of the Slave dealers, the British Commissioners say in their Report for this year;—

"In our anxiety to furnish a correct and full Report of these illegal transactions, we have not neglected any means for obtaining information; notwithstanding which, we have ample reason to fear, that many instances of successful slave importations have baffled our enquiries."—*Class A*, 1847, *p.* 184.

Some idea may be formed of the general disregard of the laws nominally in force against the Slave trade in Brazil, from the fact, that the Commissioners ascertained the landing of 13,459 slaves within the province of Rio de Janeiro alone, brought by 36 vessels; and they say, "No doubt the suffering and consequent loss of life amongst these unfortunate Africans, crammed into small and bad vessels, and exposed to all kinds of lawless acts, could it be ascertained, would be found to reach to the usual calamitous extent."—*Ibid p.* 185. The average price of the newly imported slaves in Rio, during this year, was £55 cash, and £77 in payments of three annual instalments.

In the other ports of Brazil, the same system as we have before alluded to was pursued, and slavers were permitted to land their cargoes of wretched human beings, with the full knowledge of the government officers, who most generally were implicated in it by the reception of bribes. The British Consul at Paraiba, in his Report to his government, mentions the following circumstance, showing the depraved state of feeling existing among those engaged in, or abetting this abominable traffic.

"About 170 contraband slaves have been introduced into the province, under the following circumstances. A Brazilian vessel, laden with slaves, bound to Pernambuco, was boarded and brought to, off the fishing village of Pitimbu, by a number of jangadeiros or fishermen, who, having plundered her of all her provisions, obliged her to land her slaves. I have been credibly informed, that when landed, these slaves were in sound health and good condition, yet horrible to relate, 39 of the number were suffered to perish of starvation on the beach; the remainder were kidnapped by different persons, principally government authorities."—*Class B*, 1847, *p.* 280.

We have seen that, in 1844, the Slave trade to Cuba had considerably increased, the number of slaves imported there, having amounted to 10,000 over the year before; but in this year, the island was visited with long continued and severe drought, succeeded by a tremendous and most destructive hurricane, and the two together almost ruined the coffee plantations, and greatly injured the sugar cane. The former have never recovered from the injury sustained, and the export of coffee from that island is now very small. The export of sugar, which, in 1844 had amounted to the enormous bulk of 847,000 boxes, or 169,400 tons, five boxes being equal to a ton, fell off in 1845 to 365,921¾ boxes, or a little more than 73,184 tons. The losses of the planters, and the increased difficulties of the sugar culture, in consequence of the disasters of the preceding year, and the large number of slaves thrown out of employ, by the ruin of so many of the coffee grounds, diminished materially the price of slaves, and removed the demand for new importations. In addition to these causes, the conduct of the governor and the action of his subordinates, in relation to the trade, was vascillating and uncertain; sometimes they connived at it as had been usual, and at other times refused to allow, and even took pains to counteract it. The Spanish Cortez had passed a law, professedly for the purpose of destroying the Slave trade to that island, but the Governor General declined publishing it, and on all occasions manifested the most determined hostility to any interference with that trade, except such as he might choose to originate himself. From these causes there was an extraordinary diminution in the African slave traffic with Cuba in 1845, the number of newly imported slaves being only about 1300, a fact which conclusively proves the dependence of the trade upon the demand for the product of slave labour. "These 1300 slaves were brought over in six vessels; while during the year, thirteen vessels left the island for Africa, suspected of being engaged for the trade."—*Class A*, 1847, *p.* 110.

But little change took place on the African coast, in regard to the collection and embarkation of slaves. The destruction of the barracoons and slave factories, at Ponte da Linha, Cabinda, and Ambriz, in 1843, had caused almost ruinous losses to the Slave dealers; but, as that mode of breaking up the trade had been declared illegal, it had speedily revived, and these again became places of great resort. The coast lying between the southern shore of the Congo River and Ambriz, continued to afford favourite haunts for the slave dealers; and it was to Ambriz that the American vessels generally sailed with their cargoes of "goods for the coast;" and there and at Cabenda, their vessels were transferred for the time being, or by actual sale, to the Brazilians, who loaded them with slaves, and navigated them back to the market in Brazil.

The professions of the Portuguese government, proved to be either insincere, or the officers in most of their African possessions on the east coast, disregarded them. At Quillimane and Inhambane, the trade continued to be unrestrained, and the greatest facilities were afforded for its prosecution within their limits; and, notwithstanding the Governor of Mozambique showed his good will to the cause, by authorizing the British Commander on that station, to destroy any vessel found engaged in the illicit trade, in any port or river under the sovereignty of Portugal, where no responsible Portuguese authorities resided; yet the slavers managed to overcome or elude all obstacles placed in their way, and not only were cargoes of unhappy victims carried across the channel to Madagascar, but many succeeded in making transatlantic voyages. Nearly all *transatlantic* Slave trade had, however, ceased further north from the dominions of the Imaum of Muscat.

The following extracts serve to show the deep interest continued to be taken by American citizens, in the profits and guilt of the trade.

"In January, Her Majesty's Steam Frigate 'Penelope,' found three empty American schooners, concealed in the creeks of the Rio Pongas, under very suspicious circumstances. In the same month an American vessel, called the 'Atalanta,' was transferred at Cape Mount, where a cargo of slaves was immediately shipped,—the American crew quitting the 'Atalanta' on one side, as the slaves were sent up the other. The 'Atala' and some other vessels condemned in these courts, are supposed to have been delivered by the Americans in a similar manner, and the practice is notorious."—*Class A*, 1847, *p.* 9.

Extract from a letter from Commander Bosanquet to Commodore Jones, dated Cabinda, July 2d, 1845.

"I have been particular in describing my proceedings with respect to the schooner, D. E. Wilson, to prove to you, Sir, how impossible it is, with every exertion on the part of the cruizers in this division of the station, to check the Slave trade to any extent, whilst it is openly carried on under the protection of the American flag, thus fraudulently assumed; as these vessels are all virtually sold before they arrive on the coast; and this is only one of the numerous instances that are constantly occurring at Cabinda, of this trade being thus protected." * * *

"Besides the American vessels bought by the Spaniards and Brazilians as slave vessels, there are many other American vessels that are chartered exclusively, to bring a full cargo of slave goods from Rio Janeiro to Cabinda, and from which, upwards of 1000 tons of slave goods were landed, during April and May of the present year at this port; a place where none but the slave trade is carried on. These cargoes were landed from the barques 'Pilot' and 'Pons,' of Boston and Philadelphia, and the brig 'Janet,' and schooner D. E. Wilson, of Baltimore."—*Class A*, 1845, *p*. 138.

Extract from a letter of Captain Wyville to Rear Admiral Percy, dated "Cleopatra," Simons' Bay, May 10th, 1845.

"The American flag is also abused here, as in the case of the 'Kentucky,' that was sold to the Brazilians at Rio de Janeiro, was navigated by the Americans to Inhambane, making use of the American flag, and having on board the Brazilian crew to take her back again with slaves, which they succeeded in doing about last September. The American crew that brought the 'Kentucky' to Inhambane, returned to Rio de Janeiro in the American vessel 'Porpoise,' that vessel having entered the harbours of Quillimane and Inhambane, both of which by treaty they are excluded from. It is supposed that the agent that collected the slaves at Inhambane last year, (Rodrigoes,) will try again to accomplish his object in the same manner, by the use of the American flag."—*Class A*, 1845, *page* 96.

Extract from a communication from Commander Bosanquet to Commodore Jones, dated June 12th, 1844.

"From the information I have been able to obtain, and from my own observation, it appears that a very great portion of the Slave trade, particularly from Cabinda, is now carried on under the protection of the American flag, with impunity, as no American vessel of war has made her appearance on this part of the coast for a long time, if at all; and I fear that the increase of our squadron will be found quite inadequate to decrease the Slave trade, as long as American vessels can carry it on openly, without punishment, as they keep the American flag flying after they have all the slave equipments on board, and until the moment of sailing with the slaves, when they either remove the flag and papers from the vessel, or destroy them at the time of capture.—*Class A*, 1845, *page* 28.

The following from the Reports of the British Commissioners at Rio, and of the Consul at Bahia, is to the same effect.

"We have in previous Reports denounced and fully explained the manner by which the American flag is made subservient to the nefarious acts of Slave dealers, and we lament to add, that the system of chartering vessels navigated under that flag, a system which proves the main channel for the Brazilian slave-trade was in full operation during the year 1845, and has been pursued even to a greater extent, since the commencement of the present year (1846.)"—*Class A*, 1847, *p.* 184.

"I have the honour to make known to your Lordship, that the American schooner-brig 'Washington Barge,' Capt. Thomas Duling, sailed with a general cargo, for the coast of Africa, on the 1st of December last, and returned to this port on the 20th inst., under the name of 'Fantisma,' Gonsalves master, with the Brazilian flag, and is reported to have landed in the neighbourhood upwards of 600 slaves.—*Class B*, 1845, *p.* 426.

This Captain Duling was afterwards, on his return to the United States, tried for being engaged in the slave trade, and acquitted.

There were a few vessels sent in 1845, by the Commanders of the naval force of the United States on the coast of Africa, to the United States, for trial.

In relation to the measures adopted by different governments, for the abolition of the Slave trade during 1845, we may observe, that the High Germanic Diet passed a Resolution, making the Slave trade piracy to any of its subjects, punishable on conviction with the same punishment as man stealing.

In this year proposals were made by the four powers, which

in 1842 had ratified the treaty for the final abolition of the Slave Trade; to Belgium, Greece, and Hanover, to accede to the stipulation of the said treaty, "in order, says the British Minister in his note, that it might be seen by all, that there was not in Europe a single Christian state, whose flag is known upon the seas, that has not openly and formally condemned the traffic, and so far as lies in its power, guarded that flag from being abused, for the protection of the lawless men who embark in it."

A convention also was agreed on between Great Britain and France, in 1845, by which each power engaged to maintain on the west coast of Africa, a combined force of not less than twenty-six vessels of each nation.

1846.

It is evident that, notwithstanding the efforts made by England, France, Portugal, and the United States, by keeping an armed police stationed around the west and east coasts of Africa, to prevent the embarkation of slaves, and intercept the vessels loaded with them in their attempts to leave the coast, that not a great deal had been effected towards arresting the trade, or preventing or ameliorating the dreadful sufferings and cruelties attendant on it. The native chiefs of Africa, having acquired a taste for articles of European manufacture, and finding that the flesh and bones of their own subjects, and of those whom they could kidnap from neighbouring tribes, afforded them the readiest means for procuring what they had learned to consider as necessary, continued to send or bring coffles of suffering captives to the coast, to be there lodged in barracoons, and kept until an opportunity occurred to barter them to the white slave dealer, for rum, fire-arms, powder and calico. Wherever this trade was carried on, it necessarily paralyzed or destroyed all legitimate commerce, and the poor Africans were afraid to congregate together, for the purpose of buying and selling, lest they should expose themselves to be entrapped and carried away. In one of the communications to the Earl of Aberdeen, dated May 12, 1846, we find it stated, "It is well known that every disposition existed on the part of the natives to trade, but that they were deterred from doing so, in consequence of the frequency with which the blacks, who were bearers of merchandize, (burdens being necessarily carried in that part of the country by human beings) were fallen upon, seized, and sold to the Slave dealers."—*Class B*, 1847, *p.* 85.

Where, however, they could feel secure under the protection of those whose power was sufficient, and was exerted to prevent the Slave trade, they soon evinced a willingness to resume their original habits, and engage in traffic one with another, and with foreigners, in the manufactures and agricultural productions of the country. This was exemplified among those tribes who had entered into treaties with Great Britain, and who were so situated as to be in some measure under the protection of her colonial authorities, and by this means her legitimate commerce with Africa was greatly increased: and from a Portuguese paper, called the Diario de Governo, of the 2d of fifth month, 1846, we are furnished with the following extract, showing the same thing.

"From official communications, received from the Province of Mozambique, under date of 29th of December last, it appears that perfect tranquillity reigned there, and also that the ancient fair of Mossuril had been re-established, to which the chiefs of different tribes of those districts, and thousands of the people flocked, bringing a great quantity of ivory, manufactured articles, and goats, all which they bartered for goods in demand amongst them, as articles of dress. This market, which appears to have been discontinued in consequence of ill treatment, suffered in former times by the chiefs of these tribes, has been renewed through the exertions of the Governor General of the Province, &c."—*Ibid.*

But in nearly all the other parts of the possessions of Portugal, on the coast of Africa, the Slave trade continued in 1846 to be carried on as heretofore, with an activity varying only with the demand for slaves in the markets of the western world. The trade was also again revived in the settlements of Senegal and Goree, and at the mouth of the Gambia, all claimed as belonging to the French; and in most of the places heretofore noticed as the resort of slaves, but little change appears to have been effected, notwithstanding the number of vessels yearly captured, the most of which were broken up. Every stratagem was resorted to by the resident and other slave dealers, to elude the watch kept on the coast, and to persevere in their efforts to carry on their abominable trade. One of them, during the thick, cloudy weather, accompanying the rains, resorted to the expedient of taking out the masts of his schooner, shipped about 200 slaves on board of her at Sherbro, and then, during a fog, immediately, by means of oars, got clear away beyond the usual cruizing ground, where he re-shipped his masts, which he had towing astern of his vessel. By this means he succeeded in carrying his cargo to Brazil, and was soon again on the coast.—*Pages* 2–3.

From the eastern coast we learn, by the Report of the Commissioners at Cape Town, "that the Slave trade, during 1846, has been carried on to about the same extent as the preceding year. Ibo and Pomba, to the north of Quillemane, being the principal places of resort."—*Class A*, 1848, *p.* 122.

There was, however, one change noticed in the trade, which was the absence of Spanish vessels among those engaged in it during this year. The Commissioners at Sierra Leone, in their Report, refer to this fact as follows:

"Whether the late distracted state of Cuba, and the fear of increasing the slave population in that island, may have produced the unprecedented calm in their favourite trade, or whether the promulgation of the stringent penal act of the Cortez, at Madrid, may have caused this unexpected calm, we know not; but not a single Spanish vessel has been brought into this port during the past year, nor have we heard that any Spanish slaver has been seen on the coast during that period. This cessation from the Slave trade, on the part of Spain, forms a new and interesting era in the suppression of this inhuman traffic."—*Class A*, 1848, *p.* 3.

The Report for this year, of the Commissioners at Havana, would also lead to the belief, that the subjects and vessels of Spain had relinquished the trade, and left it to be carried on almost exclusively by Brazilians and Americans. They say, "on consideration of this list, [list of vessels despatched in 1845 from that port] showing as it does, that in 1845 there were 13 vessels despatched hence, intended for the Slave trade, and with the remembrance that our list for the year preceding showed 18 vessels, the first observation we have to make is respecting the extraordinary and unprecedented fact, that we have not to record the departure of any single vessel hence during the last year, suspected of being intended for the Slave trade. This is a fact as gratifying as it is extraordinary."—*Class A*, 1848, *p.* 65.

And again, "as our list of arrivals of slave vessels in 1846, shows only four to have been reported during the year, of which two were doubtful reports, and all those in the first half of the year; the further prosecution of the trade has been for the present given up."—*Ibid p.* 65.

But it appears, from evidence derived from reliable sources, that notwithstanding this improvement, there was yet some Slave trade carried on with the Island of Cuba, and that at least 1700 slaves were introduced into it during 1846.—*Report to H. C., page* 3.

We have noticed in our account of 1845, the great depression of the sugar trade in that year, and the falling off in the production of that article, of more than one half, arising in great measure from the effects of long continued drought and a destructive tornado in 1844.

Previous to the year 1845, foreign sugars were excluded from Great Britain, by prohibitory duties, but in the latter part of that year, an exception was made in favour of sugars produced by free labour. But in 1846, "the Sugar Act," as it is now commonly called, was passed by the British government, admitting, for home consumption, sugars produced in all countries, without distinguishing between slave and free labour, upon a certain scale of duties. An impetus was thereby given to the cultivation of the cane, which has since carried it far beyond any thing to which it had before attained.

During the autumn of 1846 the island of Cuba was again visited by a destructive hurricane, which, though not so disastrous nor so extensive as that of 1844, was yet productive of much injury to the sugar crop, and totally destroyed many more coffee plantations; yet the export of sugar in 1846, reached to 810,463 boxes, or 162,093¾ tons.

The slaves thus thrown out of employment on the coffee plantations, were hired out to the sugar cane growers, and in this way the demand for labourers was in part met, but the price of slaves was greatly enhanced.

It was, however, in Brazil, that the effect to stimulate the Slave trade, produced by the increased demand for sugar, was most affectingly exemplified.

The British Consul, at Rio de Janeiro, gives the following analysis of the Slave trade, and slavery there in 1846:

"There were 52 vessels employed at Rio, for purposes connected with the transport of slaves from Africa: of these 15 were American. A return of similar departures during 1845, contained the names of 55 vessels, but, as often before remarked, such returns are no criterion of the extent of illegal traffic with Africa, for this Custom house, like all the other Brazilian departments, continues to connive at all Slave trade transactions, and there is no exaggeration in the assertion, that in this harbour vessels are most completely fitted out for the Slave trade, without any impediment." * * * *

"So long as vessels hoisting the European and United States flags, are permitted to take freights between the Brazilian and African coasts, the slave merchants are freed from many embarrassments in the transport of slave equipments; and vessels once implicated to that degree in Slave trade, are generally found to fall ultimately under the complete control of slave traffickers, and to become the means of transporting the slaves themselves from Africa." * * * "The enclosed list of departures also shows, that of all the foreign flags, the American continues to be the most prominent in accepting the price paid for its subservience to Slave trade transactions. In the year 1845, out of 55 departures from Rio de Janeiro to Africa, 14 were American vessels; and during 1846, out of 52 departures,

15 sailed under that flag." * * * * "American vessels adapted for the Slave trade, are continually brought to this port, and sold to the Slave dealers." * * * Slave dealers often purchase foreign vessels sold in this harbour, as unworthy the expense of repair, but all their efficient and substantial craft are obtained from the United States, * * * * "About the close of 1846, a screw steamer, brigantine rigged, called the 'Cariole,' arrived from the United States. She was bought by a notorious slave dealer, Thomas de Costa Rancos, of this place. She is now called the 'Thereza,' about 180 tons burden. This vessel sailed hence, about the 22d of last October, for Africa, and before the end of the year arrived at Cape Frio, from some port near Angola, with 600 slaves. She has not since appeared in this harbour, and in all probability has, from Cape Frio, returned to the coast of Africa for another cargo. The 'Thereza' is fitted with an apparatus for distilling sea-water, thus facilitating the transport of a greater number of negroes, with a small quantity of water casks." * * * *

"In reference to the enclosed list of arrivals from Africa, during the year 1846, it is proper to observe, that most of the vessels reported in ballast, landed securely at some of the neighbouring out-ports, their slave cargoes."

"Deceptive as this return is, as to the extent and real nature of the carrying trade from Africa to Rio de Janeiro, yet it comprises thirty-two vessels, of which eleven are American. * *

"I beg leave to report the following, as the result of my constant and careful inquiries, respecting the landing of slaves in this harbour, (Rio,) as well as at Espritu Santa, Campos, Mecahé, and the anchorages about Cape Frio and Ilka Grande, during the year 1846.

During the three quarters ending Sept. 30, - -	20,000
During the last quarter, - - - - - - - - - -	15,000
At Santos, from Africa direct, - - - - - - -	6,000
At Rio Grande, from Africa direct, - - - - - -	1,500
In all, about - - - - - - - - - - - - - - -	42,500

"It is said that most of these slaves were shipped on the

western coast of Africa, and that one of the means adopted to elude the vigilance of the cruizers, was to erect barracoons at various points, and thus distract the cruizers attention from the spot, where the slaves were really shipped." * * * Twelve hundred slaves were landed between Bahia and Rio de Janeiro, from the American barque 'Pilot,' which sailed from hence at the commencement of 1846. Besides vessels under the American flag, there is unfortunately good ground for the belief, that some under the flag of France and other European states have brought over slaves."

The influx of African slaves was so great during the latter part of 1846, that it occasioned a glut in the market; but even so, the cash price of what is termed "a prime slave," was never lower than $320, or about £64, the best bargains being of course, made in disposing of such as were neither young nor healthy.

"Every succeeding year more plainly shows, that at Rio de Janeiro and its vicinity, the head quarters of Brazilian Slave trade are established. It is to the capitol of Brazil that all the surplus supplies at Bahia and Pernambuco, or in other words, that all the slaves not readily sold there, are despatched. * * From this course and the increased arrival of slaves from Africa, all the slave deposits were full at the close of 1846. This state of things gave great impulse to another class of Slave dealers, who are now in full activity, realizing great profits, by taking into the interior of this, and to the adjoining inland provinces, newly imported slaves from the different deposits."—*Class B*, 1848, *pages* 251, 252, 253, and 254.

An officer employed in the suppression of the trade, writing from Bahia, a port not mentioned in the above Report says, "I regret to say, that the Slave trade of Bahia has much revived of late;" * * * * "the arrival within so short a distance of time, of so large a number of negroes, as that mentioned in the return enclosed herewith, more particularly of the unusual, and indeed unprecedented number of 1,350 in the "Tres Amigos," has given new life to the traffic, and six vessels are now preparing, though with unusual precaution as to their fittings, for the prosecution of this nefarious traffic. The Slave trade as carried on at this port, appears to partake of the nature of a lottery, as great part of the expense of equipping these vessels is borne by casual subscribers, whose share of the venture sometimes does not exceed £20. The temptation must indeed be great, as the profit on the cargo of the 'Tres Amigos' is estimated at over £40,000. No amount of ill success would appear to deter the masters, at any rate, of these vessels from continuing to engage in the trade. The man who commands the 'Tres Amigos' has been taken six times, by Her Majesty's cruizers, but his success this voyage will compensate for many losses, as he receives near £1000 for his services." * * "The 'Tres Amigos' landed her cargo at the back of the Island of Tapaina; they are said to have been in good health, and only twenty had died on the passage, but the master and officer represent the smell at night as so offensive, that to obtain rest they were obliged to hang their hammocks outside the ship, either under the bowsprit or on the quarter; they had *no water* on board when they arrived, and only three bags of farina."—*Class A*, 1847, *page* 44.

From the information obtained through various channels, there can be no doubt that not less than 52,000 slaves were smuggled into Brazil, in the course of 1846, and that the whole of the miserable victims torn from their native homes in Africa, to be consigned to perpetual bondage in the west, amounted to 76,117, of whom 19,029 perished by casualities when embarking, and while on the middle passage.* This great mortality rests upon facts well known among those conversant with the trade, and has been repeatedly admitted by those who have been long and extensively engaged in it themselves. We could multiply instances, showing the atrocious crimes committed, and the utter disregard of the lives of the blacks, but it would be only a repetition of occurrences similar to what have been heretofore narrated. There is, however, one circumstance mentioned in the Reports published by order of Parliament, in 1847, as having occurred in this year, which we will add to those heretofore given.

* Fourth Report to H. C., p. 3.

A letter from Captain Mansel, to the Secretary to the Admirality.

Ascension, October 2d, 1846.

"I regret that I should have to inform the Lord Commissioners of the Admiralty, of the perpetration of a deed of such revolting atrocity, as I believe has never been surpassed in the annals of barbarism. Commander Young, in his letter of proceedings, informs me, that he had long watched, together with the "Styx," two suspicious Sardinian brigs, lying at Lagos, which had at length been forced to sail from thence without cargoes. He then proceeds to state, that the native chief of Lagos, finding that he could not dispose of the numerous slaves on his hands, had caused upwards of 2000 to be slaughtered, and their heads to be stuck on stakes all round the town of Lagos. This fact is stated on the authority of the master of a Swedish brig, who says, that he was an eye witness; and is corroborated by a letter which the captain of the French brig of war "Fleche," mentions to have been received at the French factory at Whydah. However horrible in character this deliberate and calculated act of butchery, it is I regret to state, not without parallel on the coast, as I was informed at Sierra Leone in July last, by the Governor, who assured me that it was from the highest authority, that 300 slaves had met the same fate under similar circumstances, within the last twelve months, in the neighbourhood, as I believe, of the Gallinas.—*Class C.* 1847, *page* 49.

However incredible it may seem, that such wanton and cold blooded murder should be perpetrated, even by an untutored savage, yet the testimony is abundant from eye witnesses, that it is not an unusual thing, when food is scarce, and circumstances conspire to prevent the slaves kept in barracoons on the coast, from being speedily disposed of, for those who claim them to sacrifice their lives, either by starvation, or by deliberately knocking them in the head; and it may be said to be a common practice to take the lives of those, who from disease or other causes, have been rejected by the Slave dealer.

6

We have seen in the Report from the Consul at Rio de Janeiro, how well known, was the continued participation of citizens of the United States in the Slave trade, and how completely it is identified with the use of vessels claiming the national character and protection, and manned and commanded by American citizens. From all parts where the African Slave trade comes under observation, the same testimony is borne, and the almost entire impunity with which their part of the trade is pursued, notwithstanding it is in direct contravention of the laws of our country, renders these unprincipled men perfectly regardless of the slight efforts made to restrain them, and the professed wish to destroy a traffic, that is denounced as a disgrace to our national flag.

The Commissioners at Sierra Leone speak of the constant employment of American vessels, and the Commissioners at the Cape of Good Hope, after alluding to the absence of all power to prevent it, say, that unless means are taken to put a stop to their proceedings, " the Slave dealers will most assuredly avail themselves of the flag of the United States, to convey to the scenes of their operations, equipments, and the means of purchasing, and ultimately conveying off their human cargoes, and will thus complete one important part of their nefarious undertaking."—*Class A*, 1847, *page* 207.

An officer says, in a letter, dated February 16, 1846:—

"I have to observe that I received information, both at Quillimane, and also at Mozambique, that several vessels were expected over from Rio de Janeiro, under American colours, or Brazilian, as occasion might suit; but so long as the American colours can be degraded by covering such a disreputable trade, it will be difficult to put an effectual check on the Slave Trade in the Mozambique."—*Class A*, 1847, *page* 47.

The boats, from one of the British armed vessels, having gone into the River Angozha, found concealed there two American vessels, one called the " Kentucky," and probably the same on board which the atrocities were committed, which we have related in our account of 1844. The crew, finding it impossible to leave their vessel, set fire to her and escaped on shore. The other vessel was a barque, named the "Lucy Penniman," and so far concealed her real character, as would have prevented any examination, had not the mate, steward, and four of the crew come forward and claimed protection from the British officer, against their captain, Mathew Cooper, and other persons who they affirmed were engaged in the Slave trade. The "Lucy Penniman" had long been notorious for her constant employment in the trade. In 1843, she had brought out and landed at Quillimane, on the eastern coast, a cargo for the purchase of 5000 slaves, for which, says Lieutenant Barnard, who at the time was at Zanzibar, the slavers have been making a great rush ever since. Of the fate of a great part of the slaves brought down to be bartered for these goods, we obtain the following particulars from the same source, confirmed by other unimpeachable authority.—*Class A*, 1847, *p.* 59–66.

Seven hundred of them were embarked on board the barque "Julia," and eight days after sailing, were all drowned on the Basos de India, all on board perishing except the captain, pilot and three men. Three hundred were burned to death in a barracoon, in which they were shut up; fifteen hundred were got off from Inhambane and Delgoa Bay, through the agency of a notorious slaver; a brig on board of which 420 had been shipped, was driven ashore, and 350 more were captured by the cruizers. On her present voyage, the Lucy Penniman had left New-York for Georgetown, D. C., and left there for Rio de Janeiro, from whence she sailed with a cargo, not merely of goods for the purchase of slaves, but of articles of equipment for that traffic; and from this cargo three vessels in the Angozha river, were supplied with the means of taking off 1500 slaves. In consequence of information to this effect, from the mate, steward, and four of the crew, (the master being on shore) possession was taken of her, and under the command of a prize master, she was sent to Mozambique, where full statements of all the facts were made by the officers and crew, with all due legal formality before the proper authorities, the master, M. Cooper, admitting their truth. She was then given up to

Isaac Chase, the American Consul, at Cape Town, who, after receiving the deposition, states, in his official declaration and protest, that after a careful review of all the papers and documents,—he did truly believe, that the said barque, called the Lucy Penniman, to be "bona fide" American property, and owned by and belonging to one or more citizens of the United States; and at this present moment there is neither fact nor evidence whatever, to show that the owners or the legitimate captain, have contravened any maritime laws of the United States of America. Some time after, a person named Alexander Riddel, arrived out from Rio, and presenting himself as the sole owner of the Lucy Penniman, which he stated was of New York, protested against her seizure and detention, and demanded her being given up to him as his property. Without further examination in the case, the American Consul gave her up, and she shortly after sailed from Rio, to enter once more, as there was every reason to believe, on her former employment.—*Class A*, 1848, *p.* 279–80.

Another instance, in which American citizens were employed in the trade, is given in a communication from Commodore Jones to the Admiralty, in which, after mentioning the capture of a steam-ship, called the "Cacique," engaged in the Slave trade, he says:—"It appears, from the concurrent testimony of the Americans, who were found on board of the 'Cacique,' as well as that of the Portuguese master, that the vessel was built in the United States about two years ago, and being named the 'Tigress,' was employed as a trading and passage vessel, between New York and Stonington, and other parts of the United States, under the flag of that country. She is said to have belonged to a Captain Sanford, of New York, who, about the beginning of this year, sold her to Mr. Sexias, a Brazilian merchant, and the last owner of the 'Cacique,' for $11,500, which sum was increased to $25,000, by various alterations and improvements, made by Messrs. Brown & English, ship builders, of New York. In these transactions, Mr. Gardner, an American resident of that city, appears to have acted as the agent, and he was looked upon then and afterwards, by the Americans belonging to the vessel, as the consignee, and as there is reason to believe, engaged in fitting out other steam vessels for the same purpose."

"On the 20th of January, George Washington Rush, the chief engineer, joined the 'Cacique,' at a salary of $80 a month. * * * * It was Rush who engaged the three other Americans, Jackson Sheet, as engineer, and J. P Morris and Joseph Hamilton, as firemen. All these now declare their ignorance of the intended slave voyage."—*Class B*, 1847, *p.* 287.

"The 'Cacique' sailed from New York in the early part of the year, and having lost her foremast, put into Baltimore, from whence, having changed the most of her crew, she proceeded to Pernambuco, where she altered her machinery, and made arrangements for stowing a cargo of 1500 slaves. On leaving Pernambuco for the African coast, the commander of a Brazilian brig of war, is said to have boarded her with two boats, joined a large convivial party assembled on the occasion, and on parting, took an affectionate leave of M. Sexias. On arriving at Cabenda, "it appears that the Cacique might immediately have embarked 1000 slaves, which were ready in the barracoons; but M. Sexias would not be satisfied with less than his full number of 1500, and the vessel was ordered to stand out to sea for ten days, until they could be got ready, for which purpose he landed." * * *

"The Americans are all agreed, that at least two other steamers were fitting in the United States, to be employed as the 'Cacique' was, the same owners being concerned, and the same agent, Mr. Gardner, employed in getting them ready. If this system is to be permitted, and American citizens are at liberty to drop the very slight veil, which has hitherto covered their proceedings in the Slave traffic of this coast, it will, of necessity, entail heavy additional expense on the British government, to provide an adequate remedy."—*Ibid, p.* 288.

Between the 1st of the fourth month, 1845, and the 31st of third month, 1846, there were six vessels sent to the United States for adjudication, one of which was the barque "Pons," respecting which, Commander, Charles H. Bell, made a report to the Secretary of the Navy, from which we extract the following. * * * * * "The 'Pons,' under the command of James Berry, was at anchor at Cabenda, for about twenty days, before she took on board the slaves, during which time she was closely watched by her Britannic Majesty's brig, 'Cygnet,' Commander Layton. At about 9 o'clock on the morning of the 27th of November, the 'Cygnet,' got under way and stood to sea. Immediately Berry gave up the ship to Gallano, who commenced getting on board the water, provisions and slaves, and so expeditious were they in their movements, that at 8 o'clock that evening the vessel was under weigh, having embarked 903 slaves." * * * "Two days after, we captured her. Her crew consisted of Spaniards, Portuguese, Brazilians, and some from other countries; and, although continuing under the American flag, with probably American papers, not one American was on board. As I could not despatch her the evening of capture, she kept company with us that night. The next morning I regretted to learn that 18 had died and one jumped overboard. So many dying in so short a time, was accounted for by the captain, in the necessity he had of thrusting below all who were on deck, and closing the hatches, when he first fell in with us, in order to escape detection. The vessel has no slave deck, and upwards of 850 were piled almost in bulk on the water casks below; these were males. About 40 or 50 females were confined in one half of the round house cabin on deck, the other half of the cabin remaining for the use of the officers. As the ship appeared to be less than 350 tons, it seemed impossible that one-half could have lived to cross the Atlantic. About 200 filled the spar deck alone, when they were permitted to come up from below, and yet the captain assured me, that it was his intention to have taken 400 more on board, if he could have spared the time. The stench from below was so great, that it was impossible to stand more than a few moments near the hatchways. Our men who went below from curiosity, were forced up sick in a few minutes; then all the hatches were off. What must have been the sufferings of these poor wretches, when the hatches were closed? I am informed that, very often in these cases, the stronger will strangle the weaker; and this was probably the reason why so many died, or rather were found dead the morning after the capture. None but an eye witness can form a conception of the horrors these poor creatures must endure, in their transit across the ocean.

"I regret to say, that most of this misery is produced by our own countrymen; they furnish the means of conveyance in spite of existing enactments; and, although there are strong circumstances against Berry, the late master of the 'Pons,' sufficient to induce me to detain him, if I should meet with him, yet I fear neither he nor his employers can be reached by our present law. He will no doubt make it appear, that the 'Pons' was beyond his control, when the slaves were brought on board. Yet, from the testimony of the men, who came over from Rio as passengers, there is no doubt the whole affair was arranged at Rio, between Berry and Gallano, before the ship sailed. These men state, that the first place they anchored at was Onin, near the River Lagos, in the Bight of Benin; here they discharged a part of their cargo, and received on board a number of hogsheads or pipes filled with water. These were stowed on the ground tier, and a tier of casks containing spirits were placed over them. They were then informed, that the vessel was going to Cabenda for a load of slaves. On their arrival at the latter place, the spirit was kept on board until a few days before Berry gave up the command, covering up the water casks, in order to elude the suspicions of any cruizer. For twenty days did Berry wait in the roadstead of Cabenda, protected by the flag of his country, yet closely watched by a foreign man-of-war, who was certain of his intention; but the instant that cruizer is compelled to withdraw, for a few hours, he springs at the opportunity of enriching himself and owners, and disgracing the flag which had protected him."—*Class D*, 1847, *p.* 128–9.

To complete the history of this case, we may state that the master of the "Pons" escaped, and no proceedings were instituted against such of the crew as were captured; and we may also observe, that in almost every case tried in the United States courts, for participation in the Slave trade, the parties have either escaped without conviction, or, if convicted, have been freed from the penalties due for their crimes, by an Executive pardon.

In relation to the efforts made in 1846, for the abolition of slavery and the African Slave trade, we may note that the Diet of Sweden voted the sum of 30,000 Spanish dollars towards the emancipation of the slaves in the Swedish colony of St. Bartholomew, and that sum not proving sufficient to pay for the 523 slaves then held there, the King of Sweden ordered the balance required to be paid from other funds of the government, and the slaves were emancipated. The English government made a proposition to the Sultan of Turkey, and also to the Shah of Persia, to issue firmans prohibiting the Slave trade in the Persian Gulf, both of whom consented to give the subject due consideration.

The Imaum of Muscat, whose dominions on the coast of Africa extend from the 5° N. latitude to 10° S., and who holds the Province of Omen in Arabia, at the entrance of the Persian Gulf, by a further treaty entered into with the British government, agreed to abolish and prohibit the export of slaves from any part of Africa into his dominions in Asia, and granted authority for the British and the East India navy to act in suppressing the traffic. He however exempted vessels belonging to himself, or to any of his own family, from search or molestation.

But perhaps the most remarkable instance is, that of the Bey of Tunis, who issued a firman, liberating all and every slave existing in his Regency, and forever destroying the right to hold that kind of property, declaring in his manifesto, that "the servitude imposed on a part of the human kind, whom God has created, is a very cruel thing, and our heart shrinks from it."—*Class D*, 1847, *pages* 63–4.

1847.

Notwithstanding the large number of Slave vessels annually captured by the naval force, kept upon the coast of Africa, by

America, Great Britain, France, and Portugal, and that by the persevering exertions made through a long series of years, many parts of the coast had been entirely freed from the horrors of the Slave trade, yet the statistics of the year 1847, imperfect as they confessedly are, prove, that this traffic had received an impetus, which carried it to an appalling extent, and that the sufferings connected with it were in no wise diminished. In order to escape the punishment decreed by the governments of Spain and Portugal, respectively, and now threatened to be enforced on those of their citizens, taken in the prosecution of the Slave trade, the Slavers which had formerly sailed under the flags of those countries, very generally adopted the plan of destroying their colours, so that the nationality of the vessel and crew should not be known. Some Brazilian Slavers had also resorted to this method, for escaping detection, but that government so openly connived at the prosecution of the trade, that its laws, although sufficiently stringent in the statute book, were, in reality, a dead letter. Thus, of the seventy-eight vessels captured during 1847, twenty were without national flags or papers; fifty-four were Brazilian, and but two acknowledged to be Spanish, or Portuguese. Eighteen of the seventy-eight had slaves on board, at the time of capture, amounting to 6,598. Of these eighteen, a Brigantine, the name of which was supposed to be "Felicidade," of $67\frac{76}{100}$ English tons burden, had 317 slaves on board, or between four and five to the ton. A schooner (name unknown,) of $35\frac{2728}{3500}$ tons, had 305 on board, or over eight to the ton. The "Prendora" of 113 tons, had 608, or over five to the ton. Aschooner, supposed to be the "Maria," of $30\frac{728}{3500}$, had 237 slaves on board, or over seven to the ton; and the little craft "Rey Bango," of ten tons, had sixty on board, or six to the ton; the others, though not so shockingly crammed as these, were nearly all of them loaded with from three to five human beings to the ton, besides the crew, provisions, and water.*

It will assist the reader to form some conception of the crowded condition of these vessels, to be reminded that the

* Appendix to Report to H. L., pages 365–6.

section of a Slave ship, first published in London, in 1788, was adjusted to the regulating bill of Sir William Dolben. In the plate, representing the section in which the just proportions are preserved, the slaves are shown to occupy all the floors and platforms, on which they are laid, scarcely leaving room to walk among them without treading on them; yet that bill allowed only five men to every three tons, in every ship under one hundred and fifty tons burden, which had the space of five feet between the decks, and three men to two tons, in every vessel beyond one hundred and fifty tons burden, which had equal accommodations in point of height, between the decks. Some of those mentioned above, had four times the number, and some even more than four times the number which the regulating bill allowed.

It is impossible for the imagination to conceive the dreadful tortures which must accompany the crowding so many together in so small a space, within the burning climate of the tropics.

The Commissioners at the different stations, on the coast of Africa and its vicinity, in their Reports express the opinion, that the activity of the traffic had increased throughout this year, and that the demand for slaves stimulated the dealers to overcome all the obstacles thrown in their way. Thus, the Commissioners at Sierra Leone, say in their half yearly Report on the Slave trade on the west coast of Africa, dated

February 9th.

"The principal barracoons on that coast, are at the Gallinas and Solyman rivers, where, between 2000 and 3000 slaves are kept in readiness for shipping; there are also barracoons at Lugury, in the vicinity of the Cape Mount territory, where the notorious Canot keeps the greater part of his slaves." * * * "Great distress has been experienced, owing to the difficulty of procuring food for so many slaves, and numbers have died of starvation in consequence."—*Class A*, 1848, *p.* 295.

And in their despatch, dated Dec. 31st, 1847, they further say:

"Although owing to the circumstance of our having no

longer jurisdiction over Brazilian vessels, and the now general destruction of evidences of the nationality of Spanish slavers, the operations of the mixed courts here, have been necessarily very limited, the number of slave cases proceeded against at Sierra Leone, during 1847, has been considerable. In the Vice Admiralty Court, there have been adjudicated within the year * * * * seventeen acknowledged Brazilian vessels, and ten others, without colours or papers. * * * These twenty-seven captures, were made in the following localities. In the latitude or neighbourhood of Gallinas, Sherbro, or Cape Mount, five; in the Bight of Benin, nine; off the coast of Loango, nine; and off the coast of Angola, four. * * * Of the seventeen Brazilian vessels, * * ten got their imperial passports at Rio de Janeiro, and seven at Bahia; ten cleared for Brazilian coasting voyages; three for the Azores, Canaries, or Cape Verde Islands, and four only for the coast of Africa. From this, it would seem, that although the Brazilian Slave Trade is prosecuted almost openly, *and to an extent hitherto unparalleled*, some sort of surveillance is still apparently exercised, at Rio de Janeiro, at least, over national vessels, clearing direct for this coast. It is understood that some few of them, (vessels without flags or colours,) were both Spanish property and engaged in the Spanish Slave Trade; the present high price of slaves at Havana holding out an inducement not likely to be resisted by men, restricted by nothing but the dread of severe punishment, which, under existing circumstances, they well know may be evaded, by the course to which we have alluded.

"So far as regards the slave vessels adjudicated here, the number detained north of the Line, rather exceeds those taken to the southward. It is, however, an unquestionable fact, that during 1847, the principal Slave trade has been carried on to the southward of the Line; though we regret to find, that of late, the traffic in the Bight of Benin has greatly increased; that part of the coast is indeed now described, as "swarming with slavers." Between the Bight of Benin and this settlement, there has not been comparatively much Slave Trade during the year, as far as our intelligence extends; and to the northward of

Sierra Leone, still less. In the river Pongos, we have learnt with satisfaction, several of the Slave traders are turning their attention to the cultivation of ground-nuts, for which the demand is increasing, and far exceeds the supply. The neighbourhood of Bissao, and Bissagos, unfortunately however, retain an infamous celebrity, and depots for slaves collected at those places, still exist in some of the Cape Verde Islands. * * * * * In closing our Report for this year, we regret to have to state, * * * that from the information which has reached us, we are led to the conviction, that the Slave trade on this coast *has never been more vigorously carried on than at present, or more successfully,* notwithstanding the great zeal of Her Majesty's squadron, demonstrated by the number of vessels captured, and of slaves liberated."—*Class A*, 1848, *p.* 14.

The Commissioners at Loando, say, in their Report, dated February 18, 1847 :—

"The number of vessels engaged, or supposed to be engaged in the Slave trade, which have been captured and destroyed by [the] respective squadrons, as far as our information extends, [during the year 1846,]" is sixty-one. "It has lately been again said, that a steamer with a full cargo had escaped from the neighbourhood of Cabinda. We have not the means * * at this moment, of ascertaining the truth of this statement; we are, however, induced to give it greater credit than we otherwise should * * * * * from the information which has reached us, on undoubted authority, of the intention of the Brazilian speculators, to employ several steamers, conjointly, with old and comparatively valueless vessels, to be used as decoys, by engaging the attention of the cruizers, and drawing them off in pursuit, with the hope of affording opportunity to the steamers to run in during the chase, and ship the cargoes. One such successful attempt, would more than compensate the loss of a dozen worn out vessels, even should they all be sacrificed, and none of them be able to ship slaves themselves." * * * *

"What effect such heavy losses as the Slave dealers have suffered for two successive years may eventually produce, time only can determine, but we have every reason to believe, *that they are relaxing nothing of their efforts to attain their object*, (of which the above intelligence may be evidenced as strongly corroborative,) and that the barracoons all along the coast are, to this day, as fully supplied with slaves as ever, waiting only a favourable opportunity for embarkation, which, in defiance of the vigilance of the cruizers is, we fear, too often accomplished."—*Class A*, 1848, *pages* 154–5.

In another Report from the same Commissioners, dated February 8th, 1848, they say: "In the course of last month accounts reached us through a source from which it was difficult to withhold credit, of the shipment of a large number of slaves from the coast, to the north of Ambriz." After speaking of a barque which had got off with no less 1400 slaves, they continue, " a still more startling circumstance however has occurred at Ambriz itself, where, on the night of the 20th ult, a large armed steam-ship embarked 1084 slaves, and sailed a few hours before day-light, on the morning of the 21st. She was subsequently met well out at sea, by an American trader, on her passage from St. Helen to Ambriz, where, on the arrival of the latter, the fact was celebrated with fire-works and every kind of rejoicing."—*Class A*, 1849, *p.* 101.

Again they say: " To your Lordship, the cause of this fresh impulse to the traffic, and of the determination on the part of those engaged in it, to persevere at all hazzards, and to spare no expense even to the fitting out, as we see of large armed steamers, will be more readily apparent than it can be to us, with our very confined means of information, in this remote and isolated spot; but the fact is unquestionable, and each day's experience confirms it more and more."—*Ibid*, *p.* 105.

From the Cape de Verds, where the suppression of the Slave trade was impeded by the corrupt practices of the Portuguese authorities, the Commissioners state that " these islands are again becoming the resort of slavers," and mention four vessels seen there suspected of being in the trade, one of them an American.

Respecting the state of the Slave trade on the east coast of Africa, Captain Ricketts says, in a despatch to Admiral Dacres, dated

Simons' Bay, April 29th, 1847.

"The Slave trade has recently increased on the east side of this coast, and some of the speculations of that nature which were carried on on the west coast of Africa, have been transferred to the Mozambique Channel, principally to the Portuguese settlements. A large quantity of the vessels, almost all of which go from Rio de Janeiro, escape without capture. Arrangements are made from Brazil, by a previous vessel, to have the number of slaves required, ready at a certain part of the coast at a fixed time, generally at the full and change of the moon, allowance being made also for a long passage, so that the period between arrival and the time fixed on may be passed at an anchorage on the coast of Madagascar, in order to ensure, by extreme punctuality at the appointed rendezvous, a rapid embarkation of the negroes, thereby diminishing the risks of capture by the cruizers."—*Class A*, 1848, *p.* 308.

The Commissioners at the Cape of Good Hope Report;

Cape Town, November 22d, 1847.

"We learn by this opportunity, that the Slave Trade continues in more than its former vigour, and that the exportations have been very numerous, especially from Angozha."—*Class A.* 1848, *page* 131.

As it is well known, that efforts are made to prevent the Commissioners from obtaining a full knowledge of the extent to which the Slave trade is carried on, in the places where they are respectively stationed, it is reasonable to conclude, that their representations of its activity and extent fall below, rather than exceed the reality.

The operation of the sugar laws of Great Britain, as we have before observed, stimulated the trade to a lamentable extent. The importation of foreign sugars into that country, for home consumption, had risen from 77,372 cwts. in 1845, to 992,333 cwt. in 1847, and the demand was increasing. To supply the market thus opened, Brazil and the Spanish colonies were striving in earnest competition, and there appeared to be neither principle nor correct feeling in the great body of the people there to restrain them from exacting all that could be derived from slave labour. Although we have seen that at the close of 1846, the markets in Brazil were glutted with Africans, yet the system pursued kept up the demand. New sugar grounds were opened, and the calculation was deliberately made, how many hours out of the twenty-four the slaves could be forced to work, and yet live long enough to make their labour profitable to the owners. The effect of this was, that during 1847, there were exported from Africa, for the western markets, 84,000 of her natives, of whom 21,000 were believed to have perished prior to the arrival of the slavers at their destined ports; 60,000 were landed in Brazil; 1,000 arrived in the Spanish colonies, and 3,967 were captured by cruizers. This estimate, there can be little doubt, falls short of the reality. Lord Howden, in his despatch to Viscount Palmerston, dated Rio de Janeiro, 9th February, 1848, says: "According to the best estimation I have been able to make, above 60,000 Africans, have been imported as slaves into Brazil during the year 1847. There is no doubt that this frightful number has been greatly occasioned by the concentration of the English naval force in the waters of the Plate; at the same time I learn, that never have the Slave dealers so perfected all the appurtenances and appliances of their vile trade as at present; never have they so organized the whole range of shore signals from St. Katharine's to Bahia, nor established such facilities for landing their cargoes as now, and I am afraid I may add with perfect truth, that never was the toleration, not to say co-operation of this government, more open than at the present moment. It is a well known fact here, that a vessel belonging to this port made five voyages to the coast during the last year, and landed in safety all her cargoes; at a moderate computation this single ship must have brought from 2000 to 3000 slaves.—*Class B*, 1849, *p*. 1.

Acting Consul Westwood, in his Annual Report, dated Rio, February 17th, 1848, gives an analysis of the African trade from that port in 1847, by which it appears, that of forty vessels that sailed from there for Africa, fifteen were under the American flag; and of twenty-seven that arrived from thence, eleven carried the American flag. After alluding to the great success of the slavers, in landing full cargoes of slaves, he says, "this success may be mainly attributed to the great assistance and protection that Slave dealers have derived from the use of the American flag, which has so aided them in organizing their plans on the coast of Africa, as to facilitate in a great measure the embarkation of slaves, and the departure of the vessels; and it is much to be feared, that so long as the flag of the United States continues so entirely subservient to all Slave trading purposes as it is at present, the suppression of this nefarious traffic by British cruizers, will be greatly retarded. The fact that the flag of the United States affords in every way, the greatest protection to the Slave trade, has lately been but too clearly proved, by the numerous cases that have occurred of American vessels being sold to well-known slave dealers, without changing colours; and there are now in this harbour, two brigs, the "Brazil" and "Don Juan," wearing American colours, while they are well-known to belong to notorious Slave traders. Besides these two vessels, the barque "Camilla," barque "Ceres," and brigs "Malaga," "Whig," and "Joseph," have lately been sold, and furnished by Mr. Parks, the American Consul, with sea-letters for African voyages.—*Class B*, 1849, *p.* 143.

The Consul at Bahia in his Report, dated December 31st, 1847, observes:

"It appears from the Slave returns, which I have had the honor to transmit to your Lordship, that 3,500 slaves have been landed in the vicinity of this city during the quarter ending this day, being the largest importation that has taken place during a like period for the last eight years. The enclosed statement shows the number of slaves annually imported into this province since the year 1840, from which it appears, that the Slave trade is increasing in a great degree; which may be accounted for by the great temptation now held out to individuals to embark in this traffic, as small shares can be obtained in the companies established here for that purpose.

" Vessels are frequently arriving from the Mediterranean and the United States, which are bought by the above mentioned companies, and sent to the coast of Africa, under the flag of the nation to which they originally belonged, changing it to that of Brazil, when in the act of receiving slaves on board. A lamentable instance of this practice occurred lately, with the American brig 'George,' which sailed hence for Africa on the 29th of August last, returning hither on the 16th inst., under Brazilian colours, and the name of 'Tentativa,' landing a cargo of 726 slaves in a miserable state of starvation; 111 poor creatures having perished on the passage, from deficiency of water and provisions."—*Class B*, 1848, *p*. 289.

Statement of the number of slaves imported into the Province of Bahia, during the years 1840 to 1847 inclusive:

1840	1,413 slaves	1844	6,501 slaves
1841	1,470 "	1845	5,582 "
1842	2,520 "	1846	7,354 "
1843	3,111 "	1847	10,064.—*Ibid.*

As the port of Bahia is withdrawn from the immediate notice of the Emperor, it affords opportunity for the government officers to give countenance to the Slave trade, and draw a revenue therefrom, without so openly committing their superiors, as when done in the immediate presence of the court; and the slavers knowing the terms to be fixed on which they are permitted to land their cargoes, have adopted the plan of proceeding at once to that place. A letter from Commander Moorman, dated Bahia, April 25th, 1847, gives the following information:

* * " The port of Ilassum and the Island of Hassarica, [on the coast of Brazil] afford every facility for the landing of African slaves, intended for the market of Bahia. A government agent attends to levy the tax on those landed, and as an average of upwards of 5000 slaves are landed annually, at a doubloon a head, for healthy males, a considerable revenue must accrue. Bahia seems a favourite starting point for all parts of the west-

ern coast of Africa. American bottoms start, generally speaking, for Ambriz and the coast of Benguela; the arrangements there being such, that a vessel may ship her slaves in a couple of hours, and changing her flag with a breeze, soon gets a good offing. It is on record, that the barracoons at Ambriz, emptied themselves of 8000 Africans in one week.

"The 'Martin Van Buren,' American schooner, has just returned hence, entering this harbour in ballast. The Genoese polacca, 'Silfido,' landed 1200 slaves from Benguela, about the 10th of March, and left this again for the coast, on the 15th of April. Some idea may be formed of the immense profit arising, as it is said she carries slaves on freight at seventy-five dollars a head."—*Class A*, 1848, *p*. 300.

From these documents it is apparent, that the importation of Africans into the various ports of Brazil, had, in 1847, risen to a most appalling height. How they fared, when landed there, we have no accurate information; but, eager as their purchasers were, to heap up wealth, by working their sugar grounds to the utmost extent of their capacity, there is strong reason to fear that the poor, unprotected, unpitied slaves, fared no better, if not worse, than when the following picture was drawn by one of the Consuls residing on the spot, a year or two before.— "Some of the abominations practised on the unfortunate slaves, I have already recounted. * * I have stated, that the condition of the urbane slaves is superior to that of the piraedial or rustic slave. I have declared the reason for this; I therefore now repeat generally, that they are treated worse than beasts—plunged into the profoundest depths of ignorance and degradation—their lives at the boasted disposal of their masters—overworked to such an incredible extent, that I am anxious, and intend if possible, to collect some vital statistics which may demonstrate to what point strength and life itself may be driven before they emancipate themselves. It has lately come to my knowledge, that many of these wretched creatures are worked twenty-two hours out of the twenty-four, goaded to their tasks, loaded with irons, diseases engendered. How is life supported?

Without sympathy, consideration, or common feeling, the very bonds of nature severed. What rest, what nourishment, what consolation is administered to sustain these onerous gesticulations ?"

Another, subsequently referring to the above, says: "Not any improvement has taken place either in the quantity or quality of their food, nor any additional hours of relaxation granted. I feel inclined to say, that these have been curtailed, the increased demand for sugar in the European markets inducing the planters to work their mills night and day, that they may take advantage of the favoured opportunity. The slave is never thought of, unremitting labour is demanded—a source to augment the profits of his harsh master."

The same cause that increased the demand for slaves in Brazil, was acting with equal force in the Spanish colonies, but, owing to the peculiar circumstances to which allusion has already been made, in our account of 1845, this demand was met in the Island of Cuba, by the numbers thrown out of work on the ruined coffee plantations. From the Commissioner's Report, dated Havana, January 1st, 1848, we take the following:

"During the last year (1847) the price of sugar has been so high, that the cultivation of cane in new lands has been carried on to a very great extent, and the price of slave labour has about doubled in value. Thus a great demand has arisen for the purchase of slaves, which has been hitherto met, though inadequately to the demand, from the gangs of the coffee estates lately abandoned, after the two hurricanes and the other losses experienced by the coffee planters. From this source it is estimated that no fewer than 30,000 slaves have been transferred to the cultivation of sugar during the last three years; and this would account from the hitherto little sensation occasioned by the cessation of the Slave trade.—*Class A*, 1848, *p.* 106. The value of the slaves tended to render them better treated."

The great change for the better, that had taken place within a few years, in the Cuban Slave trade, is illustrated in the following extract, from a communication of the Commissary Judge to Viscount Palmerston, dated Havana, January 1st, 1848. After speaking of the number of vessels arriving from Africa, and departing from Cuba for the coast, engaged in the contraband Slave trade in 1837 and 1838, he says:

" * * We may assent, to the general belief then prevailing, that the then Slave trade of this place, [Havana] engaged the regular services of about 80 vessels. There appears thus to have been an average of about 70 vessels per annum, sailing hence for the coast of Africa, of which upwards of two-thirds returned with cargoes, amounting to about a total of 15,000 slaves. This was to this place and neighbourhood alone, and as this was the great central mart for slaves, we may calculate that those brought to the other parts of the island would not exceed two-thirds of this number, or 10,000 per annum, making a total of 25,000 per annum. I state these numbers as the highest they have been rated at, believing they may have reached that number in one or two years, though the general average did not exceed 20,000 per annum."

Then, after alluding to the change that had taken place among many of the white inhabitants, in relation to slavery, he goes on * * * * * * * * *

"Under this different state of feeling, instead of there being 70 vessels per annum sailing hence for the coast of Africa, by the last Inclosure No. 1, your Lordship will perceive that there were only three suspected of having sailed in the last year, of which two were cleared out ostensibly for other places, and the third we heard of only by general rumor, without being able to learn any particulars; while in the preceding year 1846, we were unable to discover that even one vessel had sailed, suspected of being intended for the Slave trade. On the other hand, instead of 50 vessels arriving with slaves, as in 1837, in the last year, [see Inclosure No. 2,] he could not hear of more than three having arrived with slaves. All of these landed their cargoes at great distances from this city, and from the last a proportion of one-third was seized by the authorities of the island."—*Class A*, 1848, *p.* 105.

That this cessation of the Slave trade did not arise from any diminution in the amount of labour required in the cultivation of the soil, is shown from the fact, that the high price of sugar had led to the extensive opening of new lands for the growth of the cane, and slaves were in great demand at such high prices, that their owners were induced, from self interest, to treat them with comparative lenity. During this year, "the exports of sugar from this place [Havana] and Matanzas, amounted to the enormous total of 1,006,767 boxes, having been in the year preceding, 810,463 boxes, of which about five are equal to a ton." *Ibid, p.* 107.

Some slaves were imported in 1847 into Porto Rico, from the Dutch West India colonies, and a few slavers were fitted out from that island, but with what success is not known.

We have seen, by the Report of the Acting British Consul, at Rio, that the disgraceful notoriety of the participation of American citizens in the Slave trade, still continued, and we find it thus alluded to by C. Hotham, Commander of the British squadron, on the coast of Africa, in his Report, dated April 7th, 1847.

* * * "The participation in the profits of the trade, by neutral vessels, tends to increase their chance of success. The money or goods to pay for the cargo, is invariably brought over by a neutral; in some cases the interest in the transaction ceases on delivery of the cargo; but unfortunately, where the flag of the United States is concerned, it often happens that the vessel changes hands on the coast, and the sale is concluded when the Slave deck is laid. The best arrangements would be frustrated by this scheme, and the day of the slaver's sailing, rendered dependent on the temporary absence of the cruizer. Under such circumstances, their lordships will not wonder that the United States flag is seen every where. Their country produces the articles most sought for by the African race; rum, tobacco, coarse cloths, powder and arms, find a ready sale, and in three of these the British trade is undersold. On rounding Cape Lopez, the character of the Slave trade changes, and the speculation on the part of the Brazilians, is founded on

the principle of employing vessels of little value, to be crowded to excess with slaves. It is said that one arrival in four, pays the adventurer; here it is therefore that this traffic assumes its most horrid form; at this moment the 'Penelope' has in tow a slaver, of certainly not more than 60 tons, in which 312 human beings were stowed; the excess of the imagination cannot depict a scene more revolting. Vessels for this part of the coast, sail out of Rio, and its adjacent ports."—*Class A*, 1848, *p*. 298.

The matter was so glaring, that it again became a subject of an official communication from D. Tod, who had succeeded H. A. Wise as Envoy Extraordinary, and Minister Plenipotentiary from the United States, at the Court of Brazil, and who, addressed the following despatch to James Buchanan, then Secretary of State:

"LEGATION OF THE UNITED STATES,

Rio de Janeiro, October 16, 1847.

"SIR: I am mortified to learn, by reference to their correspondence, that my predecessors have been compelled to report to your department, frequent instances of the use of the flag of our country, in the infamous traffic of carrying negroes from the coast of Africa to this country. It has also been their painful duty, to announce the fact, of American citizens being engaged in this abominable trade. I deeply regret, that it is likewise incumbent upon me, to address my government upon the subject.

"The infamous traffic is yet carried on to an extent, I am advised, almost incredible. Many discreet and intelligent men have informed me, that not less than forty-five thousand negroes have been imported into Brazil within the last year. The poor creatures are not only separated from their homes and friends; but, on their passage, and frequently after their arrival here, are treated most brutally. More or less of every cargo are murdered on the voyage, and the survivors are too often used as mere beasts of burden.

"This traffic should, at all hazards, be put down; and when I inform you, that by far the greater portion of it is carried on in vessels built in the United States, and under the flag of our country: I trust you will agree with me, that it becomes us to act, and to act promptly. For myself, I will do so with hearty good-will.

"Our Consul at this place, in the months of May and July last, took sundry depositions, clearly establishing the fact, that the American brig 'Senator' proceeded to the coast of Africa, in the month of December last, and brought to the coast of Brazil a large cargo of negroes. The depositions (an abstract of which I enclose you, marked A.) represent a scene of cruelty and horror indescribable. I was informed, that the monster Miller, the mate, was yet in this city, and that he openly defied the authority of our government to arrest him. In the hope that I might be instrumental in procuring his apprehension, to be sent home for trial and punishment, and thereby, as far as practicable, wipe out the foul stigma he had brought upon our country—as well as to keep this government advised that the United States are determined, as far as in their power, to break up this unholy traffic—I procured copies of the depositions, and on the 12th instant addressed a note to the Minister of Foreign Affairs, a copy of which (marked B.) is enclosed.

"I deeply regret that I could not have *demanded* the surrender of the wretch Miller. This, however, in the absence of treaty stipulations, I could not do. I will, however, continue to solicit it until they hand him over to us.

"It will be difficult, if not impossible, wholly to rescue American vessels and the American flag from this trade. We build better ships and at less cost in the United States, than are built in any other part of the world. The Slave trader, therefore, finds it to be his interest to use American vessels. But, above all, the "stars and stripes" give to vessels, throughout the world, a protection that is afforded them by no other flag.

"Treaty stipulations with this government, binding it to lend its aid for the suppression of the trade, and providing for the surrender of the violators of our laws, are, perhaps, the only means we can resort to for its arrest. Well-guarded provisions of this nature would, I apprehend, tend greatly to accomplish the desired end."

* * * * * * * *

"The use of American vessels in this traffic, would also be materially checked by refusing sea-letters, except for the sole purpose of returning home to obtain a register.

"These several measures adopted, and then rigidly enforced, would tend greatly to arrest this guilty and inhuman traffic. The subject is one of great moment to our government, and I hope you will, without delay, give me your views upon it.

"I have the honour to be, very respectfully, your obedient servant,
DAVID TOD."

"Hon. JAMES BUCHANAN,
Secretary of State.

"31*st Congress 2d Session Senate.—Extra Document No.* 6."

Accompanying this despatch, was a synopsis of depositions taken before Gorham Parks, United States Consul at Rio, in the 5th and 7th months, 1847, from which it appears that the brig "Senator" was of Boston, commanded by an American captain, of the name of Kelly, and with an American crew. She sailed for the coast, having some Portuguese or Brazilian passengers. She touched at Ambriz, went up the Congo, thence to Cabinda, landing part of cargo at each place, and finally discharged the balance at Loango. The mate, John Miller, and crew, having prepared the vessel, the slaves were immediately shipped on board, amounting, according to the statement of one of the crew, about 914, and according to that of another, 943. A Portuguese captain now took command; and the American flag was hauled down. The slaves consisted of men, women, and children, who, one of the deponents declared, "were stowed away in the hold like cargo." The deck and hold were both as full as they could be. Seventy-four died the first night from suffocation. One of the crew stated, that there was a great scarcity of water. They were twenty-two days on the passage to Macahé, in which time 283 of the blacks, according to one statement, and according to the statement of another of the crew, 373 blacks and three white men died.

" The language of the American Minister in his address to the Secretary of State, under the Brazilian Government, transmitting the depositions of the Americans on board the " Senator," is very strong, both as regards the heinous guilt of the acts perpetrated on board that barque, and the indignation of his government at the " outrage to her flag," and her determination to wipe out the " foul stain" thus cast upon it. How he could doubt that the authorities of [Brazil] countenanced the infamous traffic, we cannot understand. He thus writes:—

" LEGATION OF THE UNITED STATES,
Rio de Janeiro, October 12, 1847.

" The undersigned, Envoy Extraordinary and Minister Plenipotentiary of the United States, has the honour to enclose to his Excellency Satunino de Sanga i Oliveira, Minister and Secretary of State for Foreign Affairs, the depositions to which he referred in their interview of yesterday, and which were taken before the United States Consul of this port, in the months of May and July last.

"This proof establishes beyond question the fact, that the American barque 'Senator,' under the flag of the United States, sailed from this harbour in the month of December last, to the coast of Africa, for a cargo of human beings; that she received on board some nine hundred blacks; that after a short voyage she returned and landed at Macahé, a Brazilian port, within one hundred miles of the capital of the empire, over six hundred and fifty souls; and that on the passage two hundred and forty-six were cruelly murdered—not with the ordinary instruments of death, which, under the circumstances, would have been a blessing to them, but by the awful and excruciating tortures of thirst and suffocation.

"The perpetrators of this hellish deed still stalk abroad, whilst the blood of the wretched victims, as well as the cry of those who escaped death to enter bondage, is yet unavenged and unanswered.

" One of the principal actors in this wholesale piracy—the mate, Miller—is a citizen of the United States, as the undersigned has been informed. He is now in this city, and is represented to boast of his security. The laws of the United States make ample provision for the punishment of those concerned in this high-handed outrage, if the guilty actors were within their jurisdiction; and it is a source of deep regret to the undersigned, that in the absence of treaty stipulations upon the subject between the respective governments, he is not authorized to *demand* of Brazil, in behalf of the United States, that this man, Miller, be surrendered for the purpose of being sent home for trial and punishment. But although the undersigned has no right to *demand*, he trusts that, in view of all the facts, a deaf ear will not be turned to him when he *solicits* the imperial government to cause Miller to be arrested and delivered on board the United States ship 'Ohio,' for the purpose already mentioned.

"The foul stain resting upon both governments must be wiped out. The undersigned well knows, that the United States will neither forget nor forgive the outrage to her flag, and he sincerely hopes that a like spirit pervades the bosoms of all, participating in the administration of the affairs of the Brazilian empire. He will not believe, until conviction is forced upon him, but that his Majesty's government will go hand in hand with the United States in the suppression of the Slave trade. Indeed, was the undersigned satisfied that the authorities of this country countenanced the infamous traffic, he should forthwith recommend to his government, an entire dissolution of all connexion with Brazil; for the people of the United States, who are governors of that happy and prosperous land, could neither seek nor accept the friendship of a power that will, in any manner, abet the nefarious crime of stealing and forever enslaving their fellow-men.

"The undersigned indulges the hope, that his Majesty's government will embrace the occasion thus afforded to speak and act upon this important subject; and he flatters himself that the answer of his Excellency to this communication may be such as will give him the proud satisfaction of saying to his government, that Brazil will lend her powerful aid in breaking up forever this abominable traffic.

"The undersigned repeats to his Excellency assurances of his very high regard and consideration. DAVID TOD."

A case very similar to that of the "Senator," was that of the brig "Malaga," of New York, which, in the fifth month of 1847, sailed from Rio, commanded by one Lovet, for Africa, where, having made use of the American flag until she had shipped her cargo of slaves, she sailed without claiming the protection of any, and was shortly after captured by the "Ferret," Commander Sprigg, from whose report we obtain the following account.

After describing the chase of a vessel, he says:

"Slaves in masses were visible on her deck. I fired a musket to reduce her sail. On hailing, I was informed she had 853 slaves, from Loango, three days out. I had been for many years familiar with slave ships, yet the miserable state of this vessel outdid all I had ever seen. It must have been the acme of endurance to them, while we were chasing, for the crew of the slaver had forced and confined all below, except the sick, and about fifty or so, girls, for six hours. I was unable to get at the horrid truths that night, owing to the late hour of capture, which allowed me only to remove thirty-five prisoners and sixty slaves. Next day I found, that with four thrown overboard the previous evening, the deaths were twenty-eight, and as many more almost dead, which I attributed to suffocation. Having fortunately filled from the rains, near twenty tons of water, I was enabled forthwith to remove 271 of the exhausted and sickly cases, which, with the prisoners and our own crew, made near 400 on board the 'Ferret,' but this was greatly aggravated by the condition, not only of these slaves, but the prisoners, twenty of whom were down with malignant fever, making our decks a scene of loathsome suffering, and calling for our best exertions to aid them. Death ended the cases of four prisoners, and thirty-one slaves, during our passage to Sierra Leone, while that of the slaver was eighty-eight. I cannot refrain from mentioning an humble individual, in the person of a liberated African boy, on board, in soothing the sufferings of the slaves whose dialect was his own."

" The capture of this vessel affords an instance of what little impediment the Slave Improvement Acts, oppose to an experienced Slave trader, such as the proprietor of this vessel, who is the notorious Fonsea, of Rio de Janeiro."* * * * * *

" I would avoid an unnecessary mention of the misery that existed, when captured, but as you are aware, that the hasty conversion of vessels, from mercantile pursuits to slavers, always inflicts a deplorable cruelty on the slaves, from the deficiencies of ventilation, and the usual accommodation to feed them, so in this case, the sordid avarice of this wealthy proprietor is to be abhorred, for he embarked one-half on his own account, with permission for the other factories to cram her to the extent of 853, charging 110 milreis each, that should reach Brazil. Had the number been confined to 550, the space would then have afforded room and a chance for life."—*Class A*, 1848, *p.* 328–9.

It has always been a favorite object with the United States Government, to encourage ship building, by its citizens, and as one means thereof, a law was passed so early as 1792, authorizing Consuls of the United States at foreign ports, to grant the " sea letters" alluded to in the despatch, from the Minister at Brazil, under cover of which, a citizen of the United States purchasing a vessel from another citizen in a foreign port, had a right to send her on a voyage, to whatever part of the world he pleased, and to claim for her the protection of the United States flag, while so engaged. This was intended to secure the ready transfer of ownership, from citizens building ships within the limits of the United States, to their fellow citizens residing in other countries. But it proved an effectual means for promoting the nefarious schemes of the Slave trading community in Brazil, whereby as we have seen, they were enabled to avail themselves of American shipping, and the American flag, to carry on their traffic in flesh and blood. The Consul of the United States at Rio de Janeiro, seeing the manner in which the provisions of this law were prostituted there, had for some time refused to furnish these " sea letters" when applied for, unless he had

* This vessel was brought over by an American Captain.

reason to believe the applicant had no intention to engage in the Slave trade. In consequence of this course, complaints of the Consul were forwarded to his government at home, which issued instructions to him, whereby the exercise of any discretionary power was taken from him, and rendering it imperative on him to grant "sea letters," whenever there was a transfer of a vessel from one citizen of the United States to another. Under these circumstances, the practice had generally obtained for captains of slavers to be provided with two sets of papers, both of which were genuine. Each vessel was claimed by two owners, a Brazilian and an American; the latter was furnished with "sea letters" by the United States Consul, while the former readily procured from the corrupt officers of his own government, the necessary clearances to entitle him to its protection. Thus furnished, the captain sailed under which ever flag would render him the more protection, at the time being, and exhibited the credentials duly certified, which would be more likely to secure him from detention and interference.

In relation to the events occurring in 1847, demonstrating the gradual advancement of the anti-slavery cause, we may mention, that the king of Denmark, in conjunction with the states of the kingdom, decreed the emancipation of all slaves in his colonies in the West Indies; the decree states, that "moved by sentiments of justice and humanity, and taking into consideration the welfare of our West India colonies, as well as the interest of the planters in those colonies; [We] ordain that the arbitrary power, possessed by the master over the slaves, shall entirely cease; but in order to protect the interests of all, and that the necessary measures may be taken for preparing for this change in the state of the slaves, the said change will not be effected for the space of twelve years, reckoning from the date of this proclamation. Nevertheless it is our will, that the children who may be born to the slaves, after the date of this decree, shall be free from their birth, but they shall remain with their mothers or with their parents, on certain conditions to be hereafter fixed."

Portugal gave further evidence, that the light of reason and the feeling of justice and humanity were gradually overturning the dark and cruel policy she had so long pursued, in regard to slavery. A decree was issued by her ministry, which, after reciting that 'the Slave trade being already prohibited by law and treaties in all the Portuguese possessions, and it being also in accordance with the true spirit of justice and equity, in which all good policy rests, that an end should be put to negro slavery still tolerated and permitted in those possessions, appointed a committee to make the necessary inquiry, and to prepare the most efficacious and proper practical means of carrying into effect, the emancipation of the slaves existing in the Portuguese ultramarine territories."

The Belgian Government in 1847 acceded to the stipulation of the treaty, signed at London, in 1841, for the suppression of the Slave trade.

But it was not only among nations professing Christianity that the progress of justice and humanity was evinced.

By order of the Sultan, the slave market, at Constantinople, was abolished. Although, says the British minister, in announcing this circumstance, "this measure does not in any way affect the question of slavery, as the sale of slaves will be continued in private, it is gratifying to observe that the Sultan and the ministers will no longer permit a public exposure of them. I hail it as a real progress in civilized feelings." Beside this, the Sultan consented that the importation of African slaves into his ports, within the Persian Gulf, shall cease, and commissioned some of his vessels to cruize in that Gulf, to prevent the traffic.—*Class D*, 1848, *pages* 5–6.

Six of the Sheiks, on the Arabian coast of the Persian Gulf, who had been in the habit of carrying on the trade, entered into a treaty to prohibit the exportation of slaves from the coast of Africa, so far as their power extended.—*Ibid*, *p.* 8.

Fourteen separate treaties were this year concluded, with Native Chiefs of Africa, prohibiting the Slave trade within the limits of their respective territories: many of them living in the neighbourhood of Sierra Leone, some on the banks of rivers, and some whose territories extend for many miles along the coast.

1848.

In the year 1848, 31 vessels, captured whilst engaged in the Slave trade, were tried and condemned at Sierra Leone. Of these, 14 bore the Portuguese flag; one the British; one that of the United States, and 15 had the flag of no nation on board. Nearly all of these vessels were to obtain cargoes south of Cape Palmas, and 14 were taken within six degrees south of the equator. Thirteen of the vessels at the time of seizure, had slaves on board, amounting in all to 5,619. Before they could be carried to Sierra Leone, 337 of them had died. One of the vessels, of but 167 tons burden, had on board, when captured, 852 slaves. The English officer, in command of the capturing vessel, finding the poor creatures severely suffering from sickness, engendered by their crowded condition, had 300 of them removed to another vessel. Notwithstanding this care, 127 died.—*Class A*, 1849, *p*. 2, &c.

Sixty-five slave vessels, of which 64 were taken on the coast of Africa, and one near Brazil, were sent this year to St. Helena for adjudication. Of these, 11 had 2,802 slaves on board at the time of capture, of which number 375 died before reaching that island. Thirty-eight of the vessels were, when captured, sailing under the Brazilian flag, and 27 were without any national flag. Of those captured near the coast of Africa, five when taken, were just north of the equator, and 59 within a few degrees south of it.—*Class A*, 1849, *St. Helena*, 157–230.

In Cuba, in 1848, the Slave trade continued somewhat depressed, yet at the beginning of the year, greater activity was displayed in sending vessels to Africa, than had been manifested for some time. O'Donnell, the late Captain General, had really no objection to the trade, yet his exhorbitant charges had discouraged the bringing in of slaves. The Slave dealers indulged the hope that his successor, Conde de Alcoy, would be more moderate towards them. Seven vessels were sent to Africa the first four months in the year, and four during the last eight months. The Slave traders were disappointed in the new Captain General, who, although he might wink at the private landing of slaves, refused to receive any fees, or to throw the shield of government participation and patronage around those engaged in it. This was not the only cause of the small number of slaves landed in Cuba this year. The main reason was, that the price of sugar had fallen, and the coffee plantations still proved a failure in a mercantile point of view. Only 1500 slaves are reported as landed during the year.—*Class A*, 1849, *under head Havana.*

The Slave trade to Brazil, had evidently considerably increased. One hundred and forty-five vessels are reported as having sailed for Africa, and 100 as having arrived from that country. Of those bound to Africa, 56 left under the Brazilian flag; 32 under that of the United States; 27 under that of Sardinia; 18 under that of France; 10 under that of Portugal, and two under that of Spain. Of those reported as returned, 27 were under the flag of Brazil; 22 of that of the United States; 22 under that of Sardinia; 15 under the French; nine the Portuguese; two the Spanish; two the English, and one that of Hamburg.—*Class B*, 1849, *Brazil.*

Some of the vessels bringing slaves, were very much crowded. One of 80 tons landed 430 slaves, and one of 34 tons 230. A boat not exceeding 10 tons, which left the coast of Africa with 50 captives, succeeded in landing 35 of them. Of this vessel, the English Consul, at Bahia, thus writes:—

"It appears incredible, but it is nevertheless a fact, that a ship's long boat, manned by three persons, and measuring 24 feet extreme length, seven feet breadth, and only three feet nine inches depth, has arrived here from the coast of Africa, in which 50 miserable children had actually been stowed, and 35 conducted hither, fifteen having died on the passage.

"It is more than probable that every soul on board would have perished for want of water and provisions, had they not been relieved by a merchant vessel, when reduced to the last extremity."—*Class B*, 1849, *p.* 79.

A large slave steamer, the "Providencia," made at four

successful voyages from Africa to Brazil this year, carrying from the land of their birth at least 4500 negroes. The United States Minister and the Consul, at Rio, both exerted themselves against the Slave trade, to the utmost of their power, and discouraged what they could, the transfer of American vessels to be employed in that cruel and unjust traffic. Two vessels belonging to citizens of the United States, were seized by a ship of war of that government, and sent home for trial, on a charge of having been engaged in the Slave trade.

Although the trade to Africa for negroes was evidently on the increase, yet a more open opposition to slavery in general, and to the Slave trade in particular, than had heretofore been the case, was manifested by some of high station in Rio.

The English squadron, on the African coast, during the year 1848, captured 100 slave vessels, and liberated 7000 slaves found in them. The loss of so many vessels rendered the trade more of a lottery than it had hitherto been; and yet some were so successful at it, that unprincipled men were still induced to run the risk and engage in it. The whole number of slaves exported from Africa in 1848, was computed at 86,848, of which 60,000 were introduced into Brazil, 1,500 into the Spanish colonies, and 21,712 were supposed to have perished.

The English Consul, at Bahia, Edward Porter, thus writes to Lord Palmerston of one vessel:

"I beg leave to call your Lordship's attention to the Brazilian yacht, '*Andorinha*,' of 80 tons burden, which vessel has made eight successful voyages to and from the coast of Africa, having actually landed 3,392 slaves at this port, receiving the usual freight of 120 reis per head, amounting to £40,704 sterling. Her first cost, including every thing necessary for the voyage, may have been about £2000."—*Class B*, 1849, *p.* 116.

The French government this year, abolished slavery in her African colonies.

Some slaves were still shipped from the Cape Verde Islands to the Spanish Islands. A change for the better had taken place in some of the old slave marts, between Cape Palmas and the French settlement at Senegal. At Bissao the Slave trade had been abolished, and the inhabitants, as we have before stated, were turning their attention to raising ground nuts for shipping. Rio Pongos was the only place north of Sierra Leone, where slaves were collected for shipping, and in various places along this upper coast, agricultural pursuits were coming extensively into favour and practice with the natives.

From Cape Roxo to Cape Palmos, a distance of 770 miles, the Slave trade was still carried on in many places; and so it was along the coast of the Bight of Benin, from Cape St. Paul to the River Quorra, 375 miles. Of the coast, from Cape Lopez to Little Fish Bay, 1050 miles, it was said this year, by Captain Drinker, that there was " not a foot of ground untrod and unoccupied by the Slave dealers." It is true, that there are points along that coast, from which slaves cannot be shipped, but they are driven from point to point, to suit the convenience of the purchasers.

During the year, the English government, through the agency of some of their officers, entered into fourteen treaties with African kings or chiefs, for the suppression of the Slave trade among their respective subjects. Some of these treaties were signed by several chiefs.—*Class A*, 1849, *pages* 251–268.

The Slave trade, on the eastern coast of Africa, is reported as having been very active, yet some considerable check was given to it, by the firmness of the Governor of Mozambique, and of Campos, the new Governor of Quillimane. The late Governor of the latter place, had absconded, carrying off with him to Brazil, 500 slaves.

The Slave trade, in the Imaum of Muscat's dominions, was diminished; many slaves, however, were still carried into Arabia, from the opposite shores of the Red Sea, and from thence into Persia, and further east.

Tripoli continued her trade in human beings, and the caravan paths across her arid deserts were still marked by dead bodies of poor captives, who had perished in being driven to her market.

1849.

As we are not in possession of authentic documents, from which we could make out as full a statement of the extent and complexion of the Slave trade, during 1849 and 1850, as we have given of the eight years preceding, we shall content ourselves with the few details which we have been able to obtain; which, however, fully established the sorrowful fact, that there has been but little diminution in its extent during that time, and none in the horrors that ever attend it.

All the Reports from the Commissioners at the different stations on the coast of Africa, not having come to hand, we cannot say at what points the export of its natives has been carried on with the most determination and success; but if we may judge from the few accounts which we have seen, furnished by some of the Commissioners, and by officers in the British squadron, engaged in the suppression of the trade, there is reason to believe that the abandonment of the traffic in one point, is only the evidence of its having been opened at another; and that all the efforts yet made to destroy it by force, have proved insufficient, the lust of gold and the excitement of pursuing a contraband trade, proving too powerful to be overcome by the disgrace of detection, or the fear of punishment. This sentiment is expressed by the Commander of the British Naval force. In his despatch, dated December 5th, 1848, after alluding to the proposition for England and the United States to declare the Slave trade piracy, and to authorize the officers of ships capturing those engaged in it, to execute summary punishment on them, he says: "there is no doubt it would tend to check it, [the trade,] but England must be prepared to maintain her present force—it will bear no diminution. She must be prepared to watch the coast of Africa, from Tangiers to the northern boundary of the colony of the Cape of Good Hope Arrangements will be made to provide slaves in other parts of Africa. She [England,] will obtain complete success for one year, being the time required to enter upon the new system, after that the ramifications of the Slave trade will have extended to quarters where legitimate commerce is at present flourishing; it cannot be considered otherwise than a question of pounds, shillings and pence. As we augment the difficulties, so will the price of the slave rise, and the profit increase, for men will always be found willing to embark in any adventure offering excitement and gain."—*Class A*, 1849, *p.*

In the Appendix to the Report, made to the House of Lords, by its Committee, printed in 1850, are the following statements.

The Commissioner at Sierra Leone, in his Report for 1849, says: "In obedience to your Lordship's instructions, I have the honour herewith to transmit an official copy * * of a return of vessels captured on suspicion of being engaged in the Slave trade, and which have been adjudicated in the Vice Admiralty court of Sierra Leone, between the 30th of June and the 31st of December, amounting to eleven, which with the eleven adjudicated in the same court, during the previous half year, give a total of twenty-two vessels, adjudicated in the Vice Admiralty court of Sierra Leone, in the year 1849."*

"Of these twenty-two vessels, * * * fifteen were captured under the Brazilian flag, and seven without either flag or national papers, and three under the Brazilian colours, had in the aggregate, 1814 slaves, when captured." * * * "The above named captures took place in the following localities; sixteen were seized within 6° north of the equator, four within 9° south, one in latitude 15° 6′ south, and longitude 11° 18′ east, and one in latitude 24° 33 south, and longitude 45° 45′ west."

The Commissioners at the Cape of Good Hope observe: "We have the honour to Report to your Lordship, that to the best of our belief, the Slave trade has been on the increase on the east coast of Africa, during the year 1849. The Reports to this affect, which we had the honour to lay before your Lordship, in our Despatch No. 15, of March the 30th last, and which were corroborated by Captain Watson, have been still further confirmed, by information recently received, though we have not been able to procure particulars relative to the persons engaged, or the number of cargoes actually despatched." * * * "We regret that we are unable to give any thing like an accurate estimate of the number of slaves exported from the Mozambique, during the year past, and that we cannot state more pre-

* Appendix to Report of Leeds Census, page 157.

cisely to what extent the Slave trade in that quarter has been carried on. * * * Our belief, however, as stated above, is that the traffic has been very brisk."—*Ibid*, 164.

In reference to the activity of the Slave trade at Rio de Janeiro, in 1849, the Consul says:

"The correct number of departures, from this harbour to Africa, during the last year, cannot be ascertained, for many vessels have cleared outwards with false destinations, while others have fitted out and sailed from the various outports; and where not only every convenience is provided for the outfit of slave vessels, but also where barracoons, lighters, and large drogas, and all other requisites for the quick disembarkation of Africans, are known to exist. But the Brazilian return of arrivals, from the coast of Africa, is even more glaringly deceptive than that of the departures, for it is notorious to every person in authority, that all the vessels mentioned in the enclosed list, have brought slaves from thence, and that they have been landed at some of the small harbours, to the northward and to the southward of Rio de Janeiro, being 69 vessels, with about 40,980 slaves, besides 10 justly suspected of landing about 5000 slaves, making a total of 45,980. Long as this list of vessels is, it is more than probable that it does not still comprise the entire number, from the facility with which many can elude observation, in these unfrequented places. At the close of 1849, there were about 32 vessels, known to be on their illegal voyages from this district to Africa, for slaves, and 18 lying in this harbour, also belonging to slave merchants, and either recently returned from Africa, or fitting out for that coast; besides which, there are many vessels employed in Slave trade, between the outports and Africa, that rarely appear in Rio harbour. So many deceptions are successfully practiced, with the connivance of the Brazilian authorities, that it is not possible to arrive at a satisfactory estimate, of the number of vessels now engaged in the Slave trade, and owned by persons resident here. For instance, it has been ascertained that the seven following vessels, all proceeded from hence direct to

Africa, though they cleared outwards and under the American flag, with which they arrived from the United States, as follows:—Last August, brig Rio de Taldo, for Rio Grande; bark Hannibal, for the River Platte; brig Imogen, for the River Platte; in September, brig Snow, for Pernambuco; October, schooner brig Casco, for the United States, with a cargo of slave provisions; schooner Rival, for Rio Grande; and without any publication of clearance, brig Overman."—*Ibid.—Rio de Janeiro.*

From these statements it will be perceived, that at the close of 1849, the Slave dealers of Brazil had relaxed none in their daring and determination, in carrying on their vile trade, and that the Brazilian authorities, notwithstanding their repeated professions of desire and intention to put a stop to it, were so generally known to countenance and protect the traffic, that it was hardly thought worth while to resort to any method, or take any trouble, in order to disguise the extended schemes organized for carrying it on. The information relative to the trade in the ports of Bahia, Pernambuco, Para, &c., is too scanty to show its extent and general bearing; but sufficient is known to justify the assertion, that little or no diminution in it had occurred since 1848, when there were about 10,000 slaves landed in the first named port alone.

The whole number landed in Brazil, during the year 1849, was upwards of 65,000; and, although a few of the citizens, in view of the evils which will probably result from such a vast annual accession of uncivilized human beings, to their already overgrown servile population, were anxious to put a stop to it, by executing the laws of their country against the commerce; yet the power of the Slave dealers, and the cupidity of the sugar growers, desirous of reaping the profits of the open market in England, proved too much for them to contend against successfully; and arrangements continued to be made to bring more of the virgin soil under cultivation, and to increase the facilities for stocking the new plantations with slaves.

In the years 1846, 1847, and 1848, we have seen that the

Cuban Slave trade had so much decreased, that there appeared strong reason to hope, it would in a little while longer, entirely cease. This happy result seemed the more probable, from the fact, that Spain had given some evidence of a sincere desire to render her legislation against the trade effective, by enforcing her laws, and also from the efforts occasionally made by the Captain General of the Island, to throw obstacles in the way of those who persisted in seeking a market there, for the unhappy victims of their cruelty.

It is true, that the demand for labourers on the sugar plantations, created by the stimulus given to the growth of the cane, by the Sugar Acts of Great Britain, had, for the three years mentioned, been met by those slaves, who had formerly been engaged in the cultivation of coffee, or in the manufacture of segars, (which manufacture had greatly diminished) or by those who had been employed by the Goverment, in working on the railroads; but, still it was hoped, that a change had been gradually wrought in the feelings and convictions of the people at large, and that that change was so inimical to the illicit traffic in Africans, that it would not be revived to any great extent. But by the following extracts, from official Reports given in the Appendix, to which we have referred, it will be seen that those hopes and expectations were doomed to disappointment:

"I regret to have to state, that the trade is certainly more vigorously prosecuted than it has been for some years past. In 1848 I could only estimate the arrivals to have been, as I believed, five vessels, and the slaves brought, about 1500 in number. In 1849 it is, I fear, beyond all doubt, that at least twenty vessels have arrived with cargoes, which, according to the numbers reported of each, have brought 6,575 slaves. Adding one-third to these numbers, for vessels that have come to distant parts of the island, information of which never reached us, I calculate the probable amount of importation, to have been 8700 slaves. These I have to state, on trustworthy information, were sold, the best lots of adults at as much as twenty-eight doubloons, or 496 dollars per head, say £100 sterling;

the inferior ones at twenty-two doubloons, or 394 dollars per head. Women and children at less, according to their respective values. Of children, there has been a large proportion brought, which appears to me a proof of the low state of the market, on the coast of Africa, as the dealers would not have brought them, if they could have obtained others on the coast, of a better quality."—*Appendix.—Havana.*

We have repeatedly had accounts published in this country, of the war carrying on in the Province of Yucatan, between the whites, and the Indians natives there; and at the close of the Mexican war, a small part of the American army volunteered to serve there, in the employ of the state authority. Of one of the abominable circumstances connected with this war, we obtain the following information from the above official communication.

"In addition to the 8,700 slaves, estimated above, I think should be enumerated 330 Indians, from Yucatan, by the steam ship 'Cetro,' which is registered as the property of Don Antonio Juan Parego, the person now considered most extensively engaged in Slave trading in this place. These Indians were sold by the Yucatan government to him, at twenty-five dollars per head, being prisoners taken in the miserable war going on in that country, and in which the American volunteers, who entered that service, and for the most part left in disgust, declared that the atrocities committed on the Indians, exceeded those of which the latter could be accused. At any rate, the prisoners were sold, and brought here in chains, and are now worked in gangs, exactly like other slaves, subject to the same treatment. It is true, that there was a form of contract drawn out for hire, but this hypocritical proceeding was intended, I believe, more to meet foreign objections than their own scruples." The total number of persons then brought into slavery, may be stated in round numbers, to be 9000 for the year 1849.

Besides the large number of slaves introduced into Cuba,

direct from Africa, there were several cargoes imported from Brazil, the Report of the Consul noticing the arrival of three, if not four cargoes during the year. Notwithstanding the accession made to the slave population, during the year 1849, there was a diminution in the production of the island, compared with that of 1848, there being but 850,348 boxes of sugar exported, instead of 1,000,341, the export of 1848.

Of the continued participation of American citizens in the Slave trade, we give the following testimony, by the American Minister at Brazil, who says, in a despatch, dated

"LEGATION OF THE UNITED STATES,
Rio de Janeiro, January 11, 1849.

"The traffic in slaves, from the coast of Africa, yet curses this country, and I fear it will continue for years to come. I regret to say, that our flag is still to some extent disgraced in this infamous trade. Our Consul, Gorham Parks, Esq., as well as the officers of our squadron, I am happy to say, have done, and continue to do all in their power to rescue the national ensign; but so long as our vessels are permitted to clear from the ports of Brazil, for the coast of Africa, *for any purpose whatever*, no regulation can entirely check the evil. I would therefore recommend, that all trade in American vessels between the ports of Brazil and those of Africa, be prohibited by law. The *legal* trade between the two countries is inconsiderable; the loss, therefore, to our carriers, would be trifling.

"I also recommend, that our laws, providing for the issue of sea-letters, to vessels sold abroad, be so amended as to entitle the purchaser to a sea-letter, only to navigate his ship to the United States. This would at all times give to our government, the security afforded by the bond executed by the owners upon obtaining their register, and to this extent serve to prevent a violation of our navigation laws."—*Ex. Doc. No.* 6.

There is not a great deal to be recorded, relative to governmental acts, for the advancement of the cause of freedom during this year; but we may remark, that the proposal to abolish slavery in their colonial dependencies, having been repeatedly made by Great Britain to Portugal, that government, in 1849, submitted to the Chamber of Peers, the project of a law for the gradual abolition of slavery in all her colonies, by which it was proposed, that all slaves entering the Portuguese territories, ports, or ships, except in certain specified cases, shall be free; and all slaves belonging to, or who shall hereafter belong to the state, shall be at once set free; and then provides for the emancipation of all slaves at the end of twelve years. From the manner in which this proposal for a law was received by the Cortez, and urged by the Minister, it was evident that a strong disposition prevailed to carry it into effect. The subject was referred to the Committee on Colonial Affairs, which reported favourably, recommending the enacting of the proposed law, and there is reason to believe it will ere long be effected. The number of slaves in the Portuguese African, and Asiatic possessions, is computed at about 40,000.

The decree of the National Assembly of France, by which all persons born within, or residing within the limits of the republic, are declared free, was fully carried out in 1849, and measures were adopted for meeting the circumstances, resulting from the emancipation of so large a number, who now took the rank of citizens, so that their rights should be secured, and they be represented in the National Assembly.

1850.

We shall confine our Exposition of the Slave trade of 1850, principally to what is obtained through the official communications made to our own government, and published by direction of the Senate, during its last session. We may, however, first give the substance of the Reports received from the British Commissioner at Havana, up to the latter part of the 3rd month of 1850. In the first, he says, "I regret to have to state that there are rumours of three cargoes of slaves having been brought to this island, and of three vessels having been despatched for the Slave trade, since those I was able to refer to in my previous despatches." Again, in the 2nd month, "I understand that several thousands, as many as 8000, slaves have been landed lately on the south side of the island, principally in the neighbourhood of Santiago de Cuba." * * * "I fear that another report is true, that the Spanish government has granted the Slave traders permission to introduce 40,000 slaves into the island, and that the Captain General has been instructed to connive at the introduction, allowing him to take the payment of three doubloons, or about £10 per head for so doing. It is said that this is with the consent of the British government also; which I only repeat to show how openly the trade is carried on, because people think it could not be so without British permission also. A large number of Bozals, are offered about now in the markets, and a respectable American settler has had the warranty given him, that a lot of twenty-five he was buying, should have permits from the Captain General, to be taken wherever they might be wanted, without hindrance or loss."—*Appendix to Lord's Report,* 1850.

We now proceed to give the following extracts, from the papers published by direction of the Senate, just alluded to.

Mr. Tod to Mr. Clayton.

"LEGATION OF THE UNITED STATES,

Rio de Janeiro, January 8, 1850.

SIR: "Fifty thousand Africans are annually imported into Brazil, and sold as slaves for life. I believe one-half of this number are introduced through the facilities directly and indirectly afforded by the American flag. This belief is founded upon my familiarity with the subject, growing out of a close attention to it since my arrival in Rio de Janeiro. The declaration is a humiliating one, and nothing but a desire to awaken action on the part of the legislative power of our country could induce me thus to make it. As my predecessors had already done, I have from time to time called the attention of our government to the necessity of enacting a stringent law, having in view the entire withdrawal of our vessels and citizens from this illegal commerce; and after so much has been already written upon the subject, it may be deemed a work of supererogation to discuss it further. The interests at stake, however, are of so high a character, the integrity of our flag and the cause of humanity being at once involved in their consideration, I cannot refrain from bringing the topic afresh to the notice of my government, in the hope that the President may esteem it of sufficient importance to be laid before Congress, and that, even at this late day, legislative action may be secured."

The following extracts from despatches of my immediate predecessors, will satisfy you that I do not exaggerate the responsibility which attaches to us as a nation, in connexion with this trade.

Mr. Proffit, in his No. 9, of 27th of February, 1844, wrote to Mr. Upshur:

"I regret to say this, but it is a fact not to be disguised or denied, that the Slave trade is almost entirely carried on under our flag, in American-built vessels, sold to Slave traders here, chartered for the coast of Africa, and there sold, or sold here, to be delivered on the coast. And, indeed, the scandalous traffic could not be carried to any extent, were it not for the use made of our flag, and by the facilities given by the chartering of American vessels to carry to the coast of Africa the outfit for the trade, and the materials for purchasing slaves." In the same despatch, Mr. Proffit intimated that such was the participation of American citizens, under the American flag, in the Slave trade between Brazil and Africa, a United States Minister could not consistently join in a remonstrance to this government, as provided for in the treaty of Washington—assigning as a reason, that "he who remonstrates on such a subject should do it at least with hands untarnished by the vile trade."

Mr. Wise, in his despatch No. 12, of February 15, 1845, said to Mr. Calhoun:

"It is not to be denied, and I boldly assert it, that the administration of the Imperial government of Brazil is forcibly constrained by its influences, and is deeply inculpated in its guilt. With that, it would at first sight seem, the United States have nothing to do; but an intimate and full knowledge of the subject informs us, that the only effectual mode of carrying on that trade between Africa and Brazil, at present, involves our laws and our moral responsibilities as directly and fully as it does those of this country itself. Our flag alone gives the requisite protection against the right of visit, search, and seizure; and our citizens, in all the characters of owners, consignees of agents, and of masters and crews of our vessels, are concerned in the business, and partake of the profits of the African Slave trade, to and from the ports of Brazil, as fully as the Brazilians themselves, and others in conjunction with whom they carry it on. In fact, without the aid of our own citizens and our flag, it could not be carried on with success at all."

"Since the despatches were written from which the foregoing extracts have been made, no material change has taken place in the mode of conducting the Slave trade. There has been no diminution in the number of Africans imported; and the participation of American citizens in this business at the opening of the year 1850, is believed to be at least as unblushing as at any former period. The important fact is thus established, that our squadrons have failed to rescue the United States flag from the inhuman traffic, and that our existing laws upon the subject have proved signally inefficient.

"It has been asserted at various times, that the Imperial government was about to resort to strong measures, for the destruction of this commerce. Some months ago, reports of this character were more than usually prevalent; but, if any new steps have been taken to arrest the trade, they have proved entirely nugatory.

"A respectable journal of this city, the 'Corneio Mercantile,' of the 17th ultimo, in referring to the Slave trade, and to the reported determination of the government to suppress it, held the following language:

"Singular circumstances! At the very time it is said the government is seriously engaged in suppressing the Slave trade, the slave dealers are boldest and most ostentatious, and the landing of slaves is the most frequent and nearest to the principal ports of the coast. Official morality is marvellously advancing."

"If the Brazilian statutes upon the subject were faithfully enforced, the Slave trade could not continue. Unfortunately, however, those clothed with their administration and execution, with some honourable exceptions, connive at the traffic, and silently acquiesce in the violation of the laws they are sworn to uphold.

"Whilst the head of the government and many of the most enlightened statesmen of the empire, are believed to consider the Slave trade as inimical to the true interests of their country, a greater number profess to be honestly of the opinion that the welfare of Brazil demands the continuance of the trade ; and, after defending the traffic on the ground of necessity, many proceed to contend that the condition of the African is meliorated when he becomes a Brazilian Slave. However repugnant to the principles of sound political economy and of enlightened humanity these doctrines may be, they are very generally entertained by the people of Brazil. When to these impressions is added the tremendous power of the prince, wielded by those who reap the immediate profits of the traffic, it may be inferred that the few who labour for its suppression have very embarrassing obstacles to contend with.

"In this unequal struggle between humanity and patriotism on the one hand, and cupidity and imaginary self-interest on the other, the influence of the United States flag is scarcely felt, except in support of the Slave dealer—the seizures made by American men-of-war, weighing as nothing in the scale with the facilities which our colours afford in the transportation to Africa of slave goods, slave crews, and slave vessels.

"It is not my intention to point out the various modes in which our flag is used to advance the nefarious traffic. The government is already in possession of full information upon the subject. Despatches from this legation, and from the American Consulate in this city, give the particulars in detail and with accuracy.

"In my despatch No. 11, written more than two years since, I suggested certain measures for the suppression of the trade, and at the same time requested your predecessor's views upon the subject, which I failed to receive. Much reflection and close observation, however, have convinced me that there is but one way to rescue our flag from this disgraceful business. With my despatch No. 28, I forwarded a copy of a circular, addressed to the United States Consuls in Brazil, soliciting information which, if obtained, I hoped would 'induce the President to recommend the abolition of all trade in American vessels, between the ports of Brazil and the coast of Africa.' To that circular, however, I received but partial and unsatisfactory replies. From the Consuls at Rio de Janeiro and Bahia, the two ports of Brazil from which the great majority of Slave vessels take their departure, I received no answers whatever. The late Consul in this city, informed me verbally, that the proceedings of the Slave dealers were such, as to baffle every attempt to trace their operations, and that it would be impossible to reply to my circular in a reliable or satisfactory manner; referring me to the fact, with which I was already familiar, that vessels bound for the coast of Africa, very frequently clear for islands in the South Atlantic and Indian oceans, for ports in Brazil, and also for the United States—fraud, perjury, and forgery going hand in hand with the commerce in African slaves.

"In the absence, however, of the information I had hoped to obtain, I hesitate not to recommend—

"1st. That all trade in vessels of the United States between the ports of Brazil and those of Africa be prohibited by law.

"2d. That it be declared criminal to sell any American vessel on the coast of Africa, unless when condemned as unseaworthy, after survey made according to law.

"3d. That it be declared criminal to sell, anywhere, an American vessel deliverable on the coast of Africa.

"The foregoing provisions, introduced into a statute in a manner not to be evaded, and their observance enforced by a squadron of light-class vessels on this and on the coast of Africa, could not fail to purify our flag from the pollution of the Slave trade. So long as the amicable relations which now exist shall continue between the two countries, large class vessels are of no service here, unless intended as floating palaces for commodores. We require vessels of light draught—particularly steamers; and none others, in time of peace, are of the slightest practicable utility upon this coast. Several small vessels may be supported at an expense equal to that required to keep in service a single frigate. The energy and prowess of the American people have placed our country's name high among the great nations of the earth, and it is no longer necessary to send large ships abroad merely to satisfy the world of our wealth and our power.

"It may be said, in general terms, that the entire trade carried on in American vessels between Brazil and Africa, is directly or indirectly connected with the Slave traffic. No one charters a United States vessel for Africa, and no person purchases one deliverable there, except the Slave dealer. I repeat it, the whole commerce carried on in American vessels between the two countries, is stained with the blood of the African, and is a reproach upon our national reputation.

"By referring to Mr. Wise's letter to Messrs. Maxwell, Wright, & Co., which accompanied his despatch of December 14, 1844, it will be seen that my immediate predecessor entertained the same views upon this point which I have just expressed. * * * *

"I believe that in no other manner than that which I have recommended, can our government cut itself loose from the responsibility which now attaches to it in connection with this subject. The mode suggested makes no attack upon honest and legitimate commerce; nor does it encroach upon the wide field of enterprise open to the sea-faring man, who spurns to earn gold at the price of blood and the honour of his country.

"The preservation of the integrity of our flag, is an object too sacred to be placed in the scale with dollars and cents. If it be not so, let all enactments upon the subject of the foreign Slave trade, be wiped from the statute-book. If it be an improper restriction upon commerce to prohibit our vessels from participating in a trade, all of which directly or indirectly facilitates the traffic in slaves, let the door be thrown wide open, and the protection afforded by the American flag will give to our citizens an undisputed monopoly in this most humane and honourable commerce in flesh and blood.

"Citizens of the United States are constantly in this capital, whose only occupation is the buying of American vessels with which to supply the Slave importers. These men obtain sea-letters which entitle them to continue in use the United States flag; and it is this privilege which enables them to sell their vessels to the Slave traders, deliverable on the coast of Africa, at double, and sometimes more than double the price for which they were purchased on the preceding day. The vessels take over slave goods and slave crews, under the protection of our flag, and remain nominally American property, until a favourable opportunity occurs for receiving a cargo of slaves; and it is not unfrequently the case that our flag covers the slaver until the Africans are landed upon the coast of Brazil.

"The granting of sea-letters to American purchasers in this country is one prolific source of the abuse of our flag. But under our laws and the instructions from the State Department, Consuls are obliged to grant them, when the applicants establish that they are the *bona fide* purchasers, that they are citizens of the United States, and that they do not usually reside abroad. No little of my time here has been devoted to the consideration of these applications. I have attended in person at the Consulate, and have cross-examined witnesses, and the applicants themselves; and with the exception of two or three cases, in which the usual residence abroad of the purchasers was known to the Consul and myself, the parties have never failed to swear in such manner as to entitle them to sea-letters under existing laws and instructions. It is a melancholy fact that, no matter what proofs may be exacted, the slave power will manufacture them to order. With the Slave dealers and their abettors, oaths are as the idle wind, and testimony is a fair purchasable commodity. So long as the American flag is suffered to cover vessels trading between Brazil and Africa, all restrictions may be considered absolutely nugatory and futile. American ingenuity, backed by the money of the Slave importer, will triumph over all the guards and checks, which the wisdom of Congress can throw around the trade between this and the opposite coast.

"Many of our vessels have been seized and sent to the United States for trial, on a charge of participating in the Slave traffic; but how seldom, except when slaves have been absolutely found on board, has a condemnation taken place. Forfeitures scarcely furnish exceptions to the general rule. Having its inception in a distant land, the crime remains unpunished, because a conviction is in a great measure dependent upon a chain of circumstantial evidence, and an intimate familiarity with the mode of conducting the trade, which are alone attainable upon the spot where the offence originated.

"Apart from the odium which the participation of our flag and our citizens in the trade brings upon our country, it not unfrequently happens that private parties in the United States become sufferers. The case of the barque 'Herald,' lately communicated to the Department of State, is an instance in point. Masters and mates of vessels are sometimes seduced into a betrayal of the interests of their employers, and become pirates, in the hope of suddenly accumulating fortunes. Might not a repetition of outrages, similar to those which mark the case of the 'Herald,' seriously endanger the peace of the countries?

"Only a few days since, the French Chargé d'affaires near this court informed me, that he was instructed by his government to ascertain our laws upon the subject of the Slave trade; and he at the same time submitted in writing the following questions: 'What powers do the laws of the United States confer upon their agents upon the subject of the Slave trade? Have they the power to prevent the transport to Africa in American vessels of merchandise destined for the traffic? Have they power of placing an embargo upon vessels suspected of sailing for slaves?'

"I refer to the request of Mr. St. George, in this place, only to show that other governments are becoming aroused to the necessity of adopting new measures to rid themselves from all connexion with this trade.

"The painful solicitude I experience upon this subject is my apology for having thus long trespassed upon your valuable time. I could not have said less, consistently with my sense of duty to my country and to the cause of humanity. I could not see our proud banner converted into a shield for Slave robbers, and the sacred principle of its inviolability basely prostituted in the prosecution of this traffic, without once more invoking the prompt and energetic action of my government in the premises.

"Nearly half a century has elapsed since the Congress of the United States prohibited the introduction of Africans as slaves into our country.

"The wisdom and the justice of that measure are acknowledged by all classes of our citizens, regardless of their locality. The North and the South, the East and the West, would rise as one man, to crush any attempt to open our ports to the importation of African slaves. And does it not become us, then, as a just nation, to prohibit our citizens from directly or indirectly assisting to burden another people with what we would consider a dire curse? Shall we suffer the influence of our flag to remain arrayed in opposition to the Brazilian patriots and philanthropists, who are struggling against great odds, for the suppression of the trade? Or shall we not rather, by one summary act, secure ourselves from the taint of this horrible business, that we may be enabled consistently, and with a moral power, which would be irresistible, to call upon the government of Brazil to rise in its might and crush the monster, at all hazards, and at any cost.

"I shall not speak of the horrors of the Slave trade, of the misery, of the wars, of the murders it occasions; neither shall I lift the veil which conceals the hellish torments of the middle passage—tortures, compared with which the most cruel death known to the law would be hailed as mercy's boon. But I do appeal to my government, as it regards the obligation devolving upon it to preserve the American escutcheon unsullied, and the duty it owes to a neighbouring nation, to cut us loose from all participation in this most accursed traffic; and I again repeat my conviction, that this end can only be accomplished by the adoption of the measures I have recommended.

"Hundreds of thousands of American bosoms would be bared to resent an insult offered to our flag by a foreign foe; and shall we hesitate to rescue that same glorious banner from the foul pollution of the Slaver's touch, when it may be done by merely lopping off a trade comparatively contemptible in extent, blood-stained in character, and in which none but outlaws and the abandoned may be presumed to participate?

"I have the honour to be, very respectfully, your obedient servant, DAVID TOD."

"Hon. John M. Clayton,

"*Secretary of State, Washington, D. C.*"

Further information upon the subject, is given in the communication from G. Parks, who had for many years been Consul at Rio, and was intimately acquainted with the schemes of the Slave dealers.

The Minister, in his despatch to the Secretary of State, dated March 18th, 1850, says:

"On the 24th of December, I addressed a note (a copy of which is herewith, marked A) to Gorham Parks, Esq., late United States Consul in this city, requesting him to give me the result of his observations relative to the character of the commerce carried on in American vessels, between Africa and Brazil. It was my wish to transmit Mr. Parks's reply with my No. 50, upon the subject of the Slave trade, but it was not received until after that despatch had been forwarded to your department.

"I have now the honour to enclose Mr. Parks's note, (marked B,) and respectfully direct your attention to the facts it embraces. The general intelligence of Mr. Parks, and the facilities he enjoyed for becoming familiar with the subject he discusses, entitle his suggestions to deliberate consideration.

* * * * * * *

"I have the honour to be, very respectfully, your obedient servant, DAVID TOD."

"Hon. JOHN M. CLAYTON, *&c., &c., &c., &c.*"

"RIO DE JANEIRO,
January 29, 1850.

"SIR: I regret that circumstances have prevented me from answering your letters of July 24, and December 24, last past until now. The pressure of business, during the months of August and September, upon me, at the Consulate, prevented me from collecting the information desired by you; and my absence from the city since my removal from office, has, until the present moment, debarred me from access to the papers necessary to enable me to reply to you in a satisfactory manner.

"The number of American vessels which, since the 1st of July, 1844, until the 1st of October last, (when I left the Consulate,) sailed for the coast of Africa from this city, is ninety-three, as will appear from the annexed paper, marked A. Of these vessels, all except five have been sold or delivered on the coast of Africa, and have been engaged in bringing over slaves, and many of them have been captured with the slaves on board. The value of the cargoes it is impossible to ascertain, as the amount of property on which duties are paid at the Custom House, by no means indicates the true amount carried over. They were all of them loaded with goods with which to purchase slaves, and with provisions and water for their support on their passage over.

"The number of American vessels, which have entered from the coast, during the same period, has been fifty-one, as by annexed paper marked B. The value of imports from Africa, excepting slaves, nothing. There is no trade between either the west or east coast of Africa and Brazil, excepting what is connected directly or indirectly with the Slave trade. The English cruizers form the principal impediment to the prosecution of this traffic; and as our government does not permit vessels carrying our flag to be searched, our vessels are preferred to most if not all others, by the Slave traders, as offering perfect protection for the traffic from their dreaded enemy.

"The first step in the prosecution of this traffic, is to transport to the coast, in safety, the goods with which the slaves are to be purchased. For this purpose, an American vessel is either chartered or bought. If the first, the vessel, having deposited the goods at the several slave factories and posts on the coast, returns to Rio in ballast, when the charter money is paid, and the affair is ended. If, however, the American vessel is purchased, the Slave dealer (if other than a citizen of the United States) finds some American citizen in whom he is willing to confide, and employs him to buy the vessel. He does so, applies to the American Consul for a sea-letter, passes the necessary examination, and obtains the sea-letter. The Slave dealer then makes a kind of stereotyped contract with this nominal owner, by which, in consideration of so much money per month, the said vessel shall carry to any port or ports in Africa, such goods as the charterer may choose to put on board, (if not contraband,) and deliver them to the person to whom they are consigned. Connected with this is a letter of instructions from the nominal owner to his captain, (if he be not master himself) directing him, provided A B, who he understands may want a vessel, should offer him the sum of —— dollars, to sell him the vessel and take drafts on C D at Rio for the amount. In case A B, who is the agent on the coast of C D, the owner at Rio, has a cargo of slaves ready to be shipped, *then* he wants the vessel, purchases it for the amount specified, and perhaps goes through the form of drawing bills on the owner here. All this transaction is gone through with for the purpose of being able to show that all is straight, if they are questioned by any public functionary of the United States, either at home or abroad. This pretended sale takes place at the moment when the slaves are ready to be shipped—the American captain and his crew going on shore as the slaves are coming off, while the Portuguese or Brazilian *passengers* who were carried out from Rio in her, all at once become the master and crew of the vessel. Those of the American crew who do not die of coast fever get back as they can, many of them being compelled to come over in slave vessels in order to get back at all. There is evidence on the records of the Consulate, of slaves having started two or three times from the shore, and the master and crew from their vessel, in their boat, carrying with them the flag and ship's papers, when the parties becoming frightened, both parties retroceded, the slaves were returned to the shore, and the American master and crew again went on board the vessel, the stars and the stripes were again hoisted over her and kept flying until the cause of alarm (an English cruiser) had departed from the coast, and the embarkation safely effected.

"I know of another case where an American captain took on board slaves and landed them three times, and was finally compelled to come away in ballast. Both the captain and the vessel have been in Rio since. The vessel was under American colours at the time.

"You can have no desire to have me narrate to you at length, the manner in which the Slave trade is carried on, or to descant on its horrors; both are well known to you: and should the government of the United States wish for any further information on the subject, by directing the Consul at this port to send home copies of all the depositions and other papers bearing on the subject which are recorded in his archives, a mass of information would be obtained, which would cause many a blush for shame and glow of indignation, at the degradation to which our flag is subjected in this Slave traffic, and the aid it affords to it.

"In the list marked A are included not only those vessels which cleared openly for the coast, but also those which cleared for small ports in Brazil, at times when some small American vessel was in harbour which could be ordered by the commodore to pursue and capture her, and afterwards slunk into some by-port, where they knew they were not likely to be followed, and there received their cargo, even to the slave-decks, and then proceeded to sea. So, also, it includes those like the Laurens, lately condemned at New York, which cleared ostensibly, I believe, for Batavia; and two whalers—the whalers Fame and the Herald—both of which vessels, having been cleared as for whaling voyages, were afterwards, in accordance with secret arrangements perfected in this city, converted into slavers when they got to sea, and were, as I understand, total losses to their owners or insurers. As the flag ship never cruises on such occasions, her presence in the harbour excites but little alarm. In justice to myself, perhaps, I ought to add that I have made it a rule to inform the commanding officer of our naval forces in the harbour, of the intended sailing of every vessel I believed about being engaged in the Slave trade, and the grounds of my belief. I have good reason to think that many of the captures made have been in consequence of such information.

"The whole number of slaves imported into the province of Rio de Janeiro, which comprises this Consulate, is estimated by Mr. Hesketh, H. B. M. Consul, (who has better opportunities for information than any American Consul can have,) for the years 1846, 1847, 1848, and 1849, to have been about one hundred and seventy-three thousand five hundred. In this estimate of Mr. Hesketh I fully concur, considering it rather below than above the mark. I have no means of information as to the whole number imported into Brazil. * * * *

"Soon after I arrived here, I was applied to to grant sea-letters. I perceived at once, what has since been too painfully verified, the great aid it would give to the slave traffic, and after consultation with Mr. Wise, then United States Envoy Extraordinary and Minister Plenipotentiary at this court, I declined to grant sea-letters for any other voyage than to the United States, where, upon the arrival of the purchased vessel, her owner would be obliged to procure a register in the usual manner. Mr. Wise sent me a very able and luminous argument sustaining me in the views I took of this subject, which I forwarded to the State Department. *An answer was returned, informing me that it was my duty to grant sea-letters.* Since that instruction was known, I have granted nineteen sea-letters to vessels, seventeen of which (those named in the accompanying paper marked C) are known to have gone to the coast of Africa, one went to California, and the other cleared for the river Plate, but where she went to I never knew. I have never granted a sea-letter, except with the approbation of your predecessor or yourself. Of the number of applications rejected I have never kept an account. Every applicant was required to bring himself most clearly within the purview of the law. How severe and critical have been the examinations, you well know. As you inform me that you intend to communicate my letter to the Department of State, I annex copies of two of the examinations for perusal. Beyond them, there will be little in my letter that I have not in substance said to the Department of State years ago.

"Furthermore, as there is no trade in American vessels between Brazil and the coast of Africa, but what is directly or indirectly connected with the Slave trade, all commerce between Brazil and Africa in our vessels should be prohibited. Should any one deny the assertion, that there is no trade in American vessels between this country and the coast, except what is connected with the Slave trade, I refer him to the evidence furnished in the cases of the Laurens and Independence. Were these suggestions adopted, you must be well aware, that not only the whole Slave trade in our vessels between Africa and Brazil would be entirely broken up, but the Slave trade itself, in *any vessels*, would receive a severe and salutary check; and no people would rejoice more at such a consummation, than a large proportion of the ablest and wisest men this country affords. The deep affection which is felt here for the people of the United States would be increased; our commercial and friendly relations would be drawn still nearer together; our national character would be elevated more than it could be, were we to line this whole coast with line-of-battle-ships and frigates; much good and no evil would be done.

"In concluding this communication, allow me, sir, to tender you my thanks for the aid you have ever so readily afforded in the execution of my multifarious and laborious duties as Consul, and the unwavering kindness you have ever extended to me as a man.

"With great respect, I am your excellency's most obedient servant, GORHAM PARKS,

Late United States Consul at Rio de Janeiro."

"To His Excellency DAVID TOD,

Envoy Extraordinary and Minister Plenipotentiary of the United States at the Court of Brazil."

Notwithstanding the clear manner in which these communications portrayed to the government at home, the great and indispensable support the Slave trade receives from its citizens abroad, yet it would appear, from the following despatch, that the subject attracted very little attention from those in authority, until they were again, as they had been repeatedly before, called on by the representative of a foreign power, to take some step to arrest the enormous evil, and rescue our country from the odium justly resting upon it.

"*Mr. Tod to Mr. Clayton.*

"LEGATION OF THE UNITED STATES,

Rio de Janeiro, June 20, 1850.

"SIR: Your despatch No. 24, with the enclosures, is just at hand.

"I am gratified to hear from your department (as I now do for the first time since my residence at this court) in relation to the abominable traffic in slaves carried on under the flag of our country from the coast of Africa to the ports of this empire. I regret deeply, however, that the interference of a foreign government should have caused your communication, or that you should have thought it necessary to have given me *instructions,* after what I have written to your department, to exert myself 'to repress the illegal traffic.'

"You wrong, deeply wrong, the authorities of our government here, in crediting the assertion of the British Chargé d'affaires, Mr. Hudson, that we 'had of late (November 13, 1849)

relaxed our rigorous measures in the suppression of the Slave trade in American vessels.'

"To acquit myself of the foul charge, may I not with triumph refer you to my several despatches, Nos. 11, 12, 17, 23, 28, 34, 45, 49, 50, at length, and 53? Justice to Mr. Parks, the former United States Consul, and to Mr. Kent, the present Consul, requires that I should, so far as they are concerned, also repel the charge. They simply have the power and duty to grant clearances to registered vessels, and to issue sea-letters to American vessels that may be transferred to American citizens at this place. These vessels may by law clear for any port in the world, or they may clear for one port and then go to another.

"When the applicant demands either a clearance or sea-letter, if he is entitled to it, the Consul is bound to give it to him, and has no power to inquire what trade he designs putting his vessel into.

"Many of the vessels of our nation that engage in this trade change owners here; hence the applications for sea-letters are numerous. In no single instance did Mr. Parks grant a sea-letter without first consulting with me. Mr. Kent, I believe, has, in one or two instances, when the cases admitted of no doubt whatever, done so. They have both held the applicants to the most rigid proof of their right to demand the sea-letter, and unless this was furnished, it has been withheld. They have been faithful and vigilant in the discharge of all the duties of their office. They should not, then, for a moment, rest under this charge, preferred against us all by Mr. Hudson.

"It is true that the *government of the United States* have not been as vigilant for the past few months in the suppression of the slave traffic in American vessels, as they had been for some time prior to the 9th of June, 1849, (the date of Mr. Hudson's letter of praise;) but the fault is not with officers of our government here.

"I have frequently urged the absolute necessity of keeping at this place vessels of war of suitable size, for the purpose of searching upon the high seas such vessels as one might suspect were engaged in the trade. The United States brig 'Perry' was sent to this station for that purpose, and while here did most efficient service.

"Most unfortunately, however, for some cause unknown to us, she was ordered home. Since her departure, which was in the early part of June, 1849, we have not had any vessel of war in this port at all suitable to the purpose. True, the frigate 'Brandywine' has been in port part of the time; but she might just as well have been at home as here, for long before she could be got under way, the suspected vessel would have made her escape.

"We have not the right to visit or search our vessels in the waters of Brazil; and without the means to follow the slaver to sea, how are we to repress the traffic? It will afford me pleasure to continue to use every means in my power to rescue our flag from this accursed traffic; but, without the aid from Congress, and from the Navy Department which I have heretofore recommended, the Slave traders, as Mr. Hudson says, 'will continue to be worried by applications from Americans to hire their vessels.' With this aid, however, the vigilance of the authorities here would worry them to find an American vessel that will dare to engage in their infamous business. Until this aid is given us, however, the foul stigma must rest upon our nation. I have heretofore communicated my views so fully upon this subject to your department, that, solicitous as I feel upon the subject, I find it difficult to say anything more. Permit me, however, to call your attention again to my despatch No. 50. This was written with the hope that the subject, if not the communication itself, would be deemed of sufficient importance to be laid before Congress.

"Be that as it may, however, since the charge has been made against me by Her Britannic Majesty's representative, that I have been less vigilant than I should be in rescuing the beloved flag of my country from the hands of those who are worse than murderers, I feel that it is due to myself that my several despatches relating to this subject be communicated to Congress for publication, and I request the President to cause this to be done.

"I have the honour to be, very respectfully, your obedient servant, DAVID TOD."

"Hon. John M. Clayton,

Secretary of State, Washington City, D. C."

We have already so multiplied evidences of the method pursued, in order to render the American flag subservient to the interests of the Slave traders, that it would seem hardly worth while to adduce more; but some of the cases narrated in the official reports of officers of the navy of the United States, employed on the African station, published by Congress, are so much to the point, that we are disposed to give a few extracts, though with the danger of being prolix.

The first is from Commander L. M. Powell, addressed to "Commodore Francis H. Gregory, commanding United States naval forces.

"U. S. Ship John Adams,

At sea, off Ambriz, April, 1850.

"Commodore: I forward for your information, the accompanying correspondence with the commanders of her Britannic Majesty's cruizers named therein, touching the capture of several vessels claiming to be American, but said to have been seized under Brazilian Colours, as Brazilian property, by the officers of the British cruizers, after the American flag had been struck; and also the complaints of some of the captured parties, together with those of two masters of American merchant vessels, the only two I have fallen in with on the south-west coast of Africa.

"That our flag is used and abused for the purpose of sheltering the African Slave trader, both here and on the coast of Brazil, is a shameful truth—by Brazilians, and other foreigners, to evade the British cruizers; and by our own people, to cover foreigners and their property from search and capture, when the latter were destined for the Slave trade. But this, though unlawful before an American tribunal, gives no right to a foreign officer to visit, search, and seize an American vessel; nor has this been the plea for seizure, but quoted to strengthen the alleged cause, to wit: 'false American papers'—to sustain which allegation, not a title of evidence other than assertion has been adduced.

"L. M. POWELL, *Commander.*

"Commodore FRANCIS H. GREGORY,

Commanding U. S. naval forces,

Coast of Africa."

The American Commodore having requested from the Commanders of some of the British cruizers, information relative to American vessels, captured by them, the following cases are given.

"HER MAJESTY'S STEAM-SLOOP 'RATTLER,'

At sea, February 22, 1850.

"SIR: I have the honour to inform you, that on the 20th instant, her Majesty's sloop of war 'Rattler,' captured a brig called the 'Lucy Ann,' with five hundred and forty-seven slaves on board.

"The facts connected with this capture are instructive, and will tend to show the difficulties which beset an officer in the discharge of an onerous duty on this coast; and I therefore beg to submit the following:

"On the evening of the 18th instant, I personally boarded this vessel, for the first time, off Ambrizette, and examined her papers, to ascertain her nationality. They appeared to me in order, and sufficient to justify her sailing under the flag of the United States. They had also previously been examined by several experienced officers, without a defect having been detected. The visit, sir, was performed with the respect due to the honourable flag she had assumed, and in strict compliance with the instructions—the brig not even having been hove-to on my going on board or quitting her. Her movements, however, having excited my suspicion, at night-fall, I placed her Majesty's sloop in a position to 'see her,' should she sail with slaves; and on the morning of the 20th, the same brig hove in sight, standing to the westward, having a moderate breeze, and under all sail. As she continued her course, and no effort to escape being made, I was enabled to board her at 9h. 30m. A. M., and was shown the papers I had previously examined, without observing any alteration. She was at this time under the United States flag. Her decks were perfectly clean, and her hatchways carefully—I may add almost hermetically—closed, and a boom-boat over all. When about to leave, a low, indistinct murmur, wrung from the accumulating sufferings of her human cargo, became audible, and steam, forced from the pressure below, visible. I 'mutely' directed the ostensible captain's attention to this, when he instantly declared the papers to be false—that he was not the master—ordered the mate to haul the American ensign down, and hoist her proper colours, Brazilian, under which flag the hatches were removed, and a most revolting spectacle exhibited. More than five hundred slaves of both sexes had been thrust below, impressed with the idea, that if they betrayed themselves by the slightest noise, their lives would be immediately sacrificed: they therefore preserved the strictest silence until the powers of endurance became exhausted.

"I endeavoured to secure the papers, which were confessedly false, but found an opportunity had been taken to throw them overboard—a circumstance I much regret.

"Many of the crew were evidently citizens of the United States—which, however, they denied; and in the absence of any proof of their nationality, I was reluctantly induced to allow them to land with the Brazilian crew. Their anxiety to avoid being recognised as Americans is a clear proof of the sincerity of that government; for they looked with dread upon the sure and certain punishment that would have awaited them.

"I believe, sir, I am not singular in my opinion, when I state that at least one-half of the successful part of the Slave trade is carried on under the American flag—but certainly not under its protection. I have had the opportunity of meeting American cruizers in the Bights of Benin and Biafra, and can bear testimony to the vigilance with which their officers watch over their flag, in order to prevent its being violated by adventurers who may think proper to hoist it, without any legal right, for the impunity it affords them ; but the number of American cruisers on the station is so small, in proportion to the immense extent of the Slave-dealing coast, that it is to be feared, unless that squadron is increased, or more extended powers granted to the Commanders of Her Majesty's cruizers in ascertaining (in these waters) the true nationality of a vessel hoisting the flag of a nation not a party to the slave treaties, the generous sacrifices of our country may be lost, and the hopes of the African philanthropist never be realized.

"I have the honour to be, sir, your most obedient servant,

"ARTHUR CUMMING, *Commander.*

"Commodore Arthur Fanshawe, C. B.,

Commander-in-chief, &c."

"Cyclops," Loando, *December* 2, 1849.

"Sir: I have the honour to bring to your notice the following particulars, with reference to the boarding of the American brigantine 'Casco,' by a boat of her Majesty's steamship under my command, at daylight on the 27th ultimo, while steaming to the southward. Between Ambriz and Mazula a sail was observed close under the land, and on coming up with the vessel she showed American colours. I sent Lieutenant Branch to board her. The master produced a paper called a sea-letter, from the Consul of the United States at Rio de Janeiro, (Mr. Gorham Parks,) granting that vessel protection whilst trading in Africa, and stating that the 'Casco' had been disposed of by one American citizen to another, in the harbour of Rio de Janeiro, after a survey—the cargo stated to be general, and bound to Ambriz. I felt doubtful as to the American's honesty ; but being in want of coal, I proceeded towards Loando, and on my way fortunately fell in with, some time afterwards, her Majesty's steam vessel 'Pluto,' and directed her commander to proceed to watch the movements of the 'Casco.'

"The next morning the 'Pluto' discovered the above-named

vessel at anchor, in the act of shipping a cargo of slaves. She immediately slipped, and the 'Pluto,' after a short chase captured her, having on board 420 slaves, without papers. I have not yet received my official *report* from Lieutenant Jolliffe, but will transmit it to you the moment received.

"I regret to say, the American flag has been made use of on many occasions, since I have been employed on this division of the station, for the purpose of affording protection to the vessels engaged in the Slave trade, so as to permit arrangements to be made by agents of the parties for the purchase of cargoes of slaves; and whenever a good opportunity is observed, such as the absence of a British cruiser, the shipment is effected, the colours hauled down, and the papers destroyed or secreted, perhaps to be again used on another occasion.

"No American vessel of war has been seen on this part of the coast for many months; and if this system of making use of or purchasing American nationality is continued, in my opinion, no efforts on the part of the cruisers will have any avail in putting a stop to the traffic in slaves.

"I have the honour to be, sir, your obedient servant,

G. F. HASTINGS, *Captain*."

"To Arthur Fanshawe, C. B.,
Commodore and Commander-in-chief, west coast of Africa."

"Cyclops, Loando, *January*, 1850.

"While at anchor in Ambriz roads, awaiting the arrival of her Majesty's steam vessel 'Pluto,' two sails were observed in the offing, which, the weather clearing, were made out to be the 'Pluto,' and a barque, under American colours. Lieutenant Jolliffe boarded the barque, and considered the papers produced by her master very unsatisfactory, but as the vessel was bound to Ambriz, he thought it right to bring the matter under my notice. On the barque anchoring I visited her, and demanded to see her papers. The master produced the register in which it was stated, she was bound to California, and he asserted she had been sold in the harbour of Rio de Janeiro, having put in there in distress, to a Mr. Frank Smith, a resident of that place, but an American citizen, being a native of Philadelphia. The master produced no document mentioning the transfer and sale of the vessel, sea-letter, nor indeed any authority for wearing the colours under which she was at the time. I informed him that I doubted his nationality—more particularly as out of the crew on deck, there was only one other American person, the rest being foreigners, and in consequence, would search the vessel. On opening the hatches she was found to be fully fitted for the Slave trade, with fourteen Brazilians on the Slave deck, in addition to the foreigners already mentioned, and two Brazilians on deck as passengers. I then acquainted the master with my intention to detain the vessel, and that I would deliberate respecting her disposal, and returned on board the 'Cyclops.' Some two hours afterwards, one of the Brazilian passengers, who now affirmed himself to be the real captain came on board and acquainted me, that, feeling it useless to evade capture, he had destroyed the false American colours and papers, and substituted the Brazilian flag, I therefore was at liberty to seize his vessel, and in consequence, took possession of the Brazilian barque 'Pilot,' of 300 tons, fully equipped for the Slave trade, and I sent her to St. Helena in charge of Lieutenant Dew.

"I found the barque 'Pilot' at that time an American, was disposed of as before stated, some months since, to Mr. F. Smith, of Rio de Janeiro, who, I hear, is the same individual who was mentioned in the sea-letter, produced by the brigantine 'Casco,' which vessel came over to the coast of Africa under nearly the same circumstances as the barque. If Mr. Smith is enabled to purchase American vessels, procure protection from the United States Consul, he (Mr. Smith) being, as I am informed, in the pay of the Slave merchants at Rio de Janeiro, and thus procure for Brazilian property the fraudulent use of the American flag, with impunity, the performance of our duty in suppressing the Slave trade will be increased in difficulties, it being in many cases scarcely possible to discern between the *true* and *false* American.

"The person (Mr. J. Myers,) who represented himself, on my

boarding the 'Pilot,' as the American master, has since informed me that he held the same position on board the alleged American barque 'Quincy,' (whom you, sir, may remember being on the south coast in June and July last;) that she was at the time boarded by the 'Centaur,' and the cruisers (*bona fide* Brazilian property,) had all the requisite fitments for slaves, and in charge of a Brazilian master, who appeared as passenger; that the Quincy shipped 650 slaves the same night that she was boarded by some of the boats of our cruisers, and that before this shipment took place they had at Ambriz embarked their full cargo of slaves;, but, the smoke of a steamer appearing in the offing, (which vessel afterwards proved to be the 'Centaur,') the whole of the slaves were relanded in less than one hour, having employed upwards of thirty-five boats for this service; and that, on being boarded by the 'Centaur's' boat, the American master and papers were again produced.

"I have the honour to be, sir, your obedient humble servant,

JOHN TUDOR, *Commander.*"

Captain Foote,

United States sloop-of-war Perry."

"Her Majesty's steamer Firefly."

Loando, March 21, 1850.

"Sir: I beg to forward you the information you requested, relative to vessels that have been boarded by the 'Firefly,' or her boats, upon her station off the 'Congo,' under the American flag. All of these vessels have taken slaves from some part of the coast or other, and, with the exception of the 'Lucy Ann,' taken by her Majesty's ship 'Rattler,' with five hundred and upwards on board, have escaped, although each of them has been boarded by most of the cruisers on the station previous to shipping, but not having the right of search, upon overhauling their papers, and to the best of our judgment not being able to detect any inaccuracies in such papers, our duty with the American flag ended. These are vessels that have been boarded by myself or boats; but the senior officer of the division (the Hon.

Captain Hastings) can give you a list of many more, all of which would have been good prizes to any American man-of-war, or officer having the right of search, for we are well assured that all of them came over to this coast fully fitted and equipped for the Slave trade.

JOHN TUDOR, *Commander.*"

"To Captain FOOTE,

United States sloop-of-war Perry."

With these extracts we close our notice of the trade in 1850. Of the number of slaves exported from Africa during that year, we have no correct information, but there is ample reason to believe, that it did not fall short of the number which was carried into slavery in the year preceding. The concurrent testimony which we have adduced of the ministers and officers of our own government, and of those of the government of Great Britain, establish beyond a doubt, the extensive, iniquitous and disgraceful participation of American citizens in this abominable traffic, and we apprehend there are comparatively few among us who are aware to what a vast extent this trade continues to be carried on, and the indescribable misery it is yearly inflicting upon the helpless and harmless inhabitants of the vast continent of Africa. The brief sketch which we have given of some of its main features, may serve to impart some correct knowledge upon the subject, and we trust will arouse a determination to put an effectual check to the further prosecution of a commerce so directly at variance with the laws of our country, and which is subjecting it to so much obloquy and reproach.

During ten of the eleven years which we have been glancing over, that is, up to the termination of 1849, according to the official information on which we have relied, and which we are well assured, falls short of the true numbers, there have been carried away from the coast of Africa for the western markets, 684,786 human beings, of whom 374,800 were landed in Brazil, and 42,277 in the Spanish colonies, while 158,696 are supposed to have perished in the transatlantic voyage. If the calculation made by T. F. Buxton, to which we have previously referred, is correct, that for every individual carried off, there is a life sacrificed before embarkation, we have the fearful fact presented to us, that within that short period considerably more than a million and a quarter of our fellow creatures, who though lacking the light of civilization, and the outward knowledge of the Christian religion, are equally with ourselves, the objects of our Heavenly Father's regard, have been either destroyed or consigned to hopeless bondage and misery, in order to satisfy the cravings of that thirst for gold, which debases the principles, and benumbs the feelings, of so large a portion of the professors of Christianity. How completely all the nobler feelings of humanity are eradicated from the hearts of those who pursue this illicit employment, may be clearly seen from many of the facts that we have already narrated; but these facts may be supposed to be isolated cases, which do not fairly represent the legitimate features of the African Slave trade. We shall therefore close our exhibit of this part of the subject, by the testimony of one who had himself been long actively engaged in the business, and to whom the various phases it presents had become familiar and apparently matters of indifference. We allude to Jose E. Cliffe, M. D., a native of the United States, but a naturalized subject of Brazil, from whose evidence, given before the Select Committee of the House of Commons in Great Britain, we extract the following:

Q. "I wish to ask you some questions relative to the sufferings of the slaves on board the slave ships, and in the barracoons. Is there much suffering generally in the barracoons on the coast of Africa, while the slaves are in the state of detention?

A. Not in the ordinary course of business. At present, from what I know, I believe that at times there is a great deal of suffering. We will say for example, that there are 500 slaves waiting for a vessel; a cruizer is in the neighbourhood, and the vessel cannot come in, it is very difficult to get, on the coast of Africa, sufficient food to support them, and they are kept on the smallest possible ration on which human life can subsist, waiting for an opportunity of putting them on board the vessel or vessels. Therefore there is a great deal of suffering now in the barracoons that did not formerly exist. * * * *

Q. Do the slaves in consequence of insufficiency of accommodations and other causes, perish in large numbers on board the vessels?

A. Occasionally they do—in many cases they do.

Q. Generally speaking is there a large mortality?

A. There is.

Q. Is the suffering of such slaves as escape death very great?

A. Exceedingly so, almost beyond the powers of description. I have seen them when brought ashore, when life has been reduced to the lowest possible ebb, when they have been simply alive; nothing more than that could be stated of them; there was a complete wasting of the whole animal system, and a mere mass of bones, but still alive.

Q. To what causes is that attributable?

A. To a long passage; to a want of sufficiency of food, and to the confinement and foul air.

Q. Is the heat of the hold very great?

A. Yes, I should think from 120 to 130 degrees, taking the Fahrenheit thermometer, and perhaps more. * * *

Q. What they suffer from really, is the fetid state of the atmosphere?

A. The fetid state of the atmosphere, and not having a sufficiency of food and water.

Q. Although the Africans would not suffer from that high degree of temperature, would it not promote a great desire for drink?

A. Of course it would, under these circumstances. Accustomed as they are from their earliest period of life to drink water, and that in very large quantities, their sufferings from want of water are more dreadful than they would be with the Anglo-Saxon race, who are accustomed to drink very little water, and require very little; but in the tropics they require a large quantity of water, and are accustomed to drink plenty, and of course the sufferings of people like these, are infinitely, if it is possible so to say, more severe in consequence of it.

Q. What quantity of water do you suppose that an African would require for his sustenance per day?

A. A boy of ten or twelve years of age would drink more than a gallon.

Q. What quantity do they usually get?

A. It is horrid almost to say; the quantity is very small. I have known from hearsay, within the last two years, that a tea-cup full given once in three days, will support life for twenty or thirty days.

Q. Even in that temperature?

A. Yes; but the loss of life must be great on these occasions.

Q. Is the agony occasioned by the desire for water very great?

A. Indescribable. There are no words that I can make use of, that will describe the sufferings in the tropics from want of water; it is ten times more horrible than the want of food. A man may suffer from the want of food four or five days and think nothing of it, but the sufferings from want of water for two days, in the tropics, are almost beyond endurance. * *

Q. Beside the sufferings occasioned by the want of water; occasional want of food, and the fetid atmosphere in which the slaves are placed, do they suffer from other causes, such as close confinement and bruises, from the manner in which they are confined on board the slaver?

A. All these causes do act upon them, but I believe that there is nothing which they suffer so greatly from as the want of water. I think that that swallows up the whole of the other small causes.

Q. The slaver I suppose, is in a very dirty condition?

A. It must be, because the slaves are jammed in, as I observed before. They are packed in upon their sides, laid in, heads among legs and arms, so that it is very difficult frequently, until they become very much emaciated so as to leave room, for them to get up alone, without the whole section moving together.

Q. Are they permitted to get up?

A. Small boys would be. Small boys are never confined, but the way in which they are put in now, is, that they are generally jammed in in such masses, even allowing that there was elevation sufficient for them to rise up, they could not rise without the whole section rising. They make two or three slave-decks in a vessel, which has perhaps, six feet between her deck and her beams above. There would be three tiers of slaves stowed away.

Q. In six feet?

A. Yes; sixteen to eighteen inches would stow them in; then the timber, or whatever you term it, of which it is built, would occupy the rest of the space; so that you would have three tiers of them in a common deck, therefore there is not room for a very small boy to sit. They are put like books upon a shelf, consequently there is plenty of room for them to lie flat, but not enough for them to elevate.

Q. Do they lie upon their backs?

A. No; all upon their sides.

Q. Can they turn from side to side?

A. By the whole section turning, not otherwise, until they have become a good deal emaciated, and some have died out, that of course makes room for the remainder.

Q. Are they so placed for the convenience of stowage?

A. Yes; for the possibility of stowing large numbers.

Q. By what means is the food supplied to them in that way?

A. By a man going down amongst them, passing down a calabash with a quantity of rice or beans, or whatever description of food may be, and passing it round, a little portion to each one.

Q. The slaves are brought on deck to feed there?

A. In a vessel where it was well conducted, the old plan used to be, to bring them on deck by sections and let them feed and wash themselves, and do what was necessary, and then take them below again; but now when they are so jammed up, it is impossible to do so; in addition to which, the want of water is so great, that if they were to see water alongside, a great number of them no doubt would jump overboard without considering that it was salt water, therefore they are fed between decks as much as possible; a few who are suffering more than the others are occasionally brought on deck, but the object is to keep as many below as possible. * * * * *

Q. The slaves being packed in those large numbers and exposed to a long voyage, after a considerable detention, are liable to suffer from disease?

A. Yes. There are cases in which the mortality is much the greatest; where they have been detained for some length of time in the barracoons, not having had an opportunity to be shipped; those are the cases in which the mortality is the greater, because their systems have been worn down previously to their being put on board the vessel.

Q. Did you ever know an instance of a vessel losing one-half of her cargo?

A. Yes, a good deal more than that. There was an instance in which out of 160 which was but half a cargo, only 10 escaped, and those 10 were sold for 300 milreas, about £37. I know that personally to be a fact. * * * * *

Q. There is one cause to which you have not called attention, and that is the nature of the decks. I believe that it has been the practice to pack the slaves away frequently upon the casks, has it not, without the intervention of a slave deck?

A. Yes, that is very frequently done, but as the African is not accustomed to sleep in a feather bed, from sleeping on a hard cask no injury arises.

Q. Do they not suffer from bruises, from being jammed together between the casks?

A. When they are first put on board they do bruise; but afterwards they become so emaciated and are so very light, that the bruising is very trifling then. * * * * * *

Q. When the food is supplied to them, is it possible for the person who supplies it to get among them, between the rows of them, or is it handed from one row to another?

A. If I were to speak the truth it would be this: the vessels are so excessively offensive, that it is perhaps the greatest punishment to which you can put any person on board. There is some half-witted person whom they generally have almost on purpose for it, to pass the food round to them, and he is in such a hurry in doing it, that those who are nearest to one of the hatchways are more likely to get a double portion of food, rather than that he should go round the sides of the vessel, which is so ill ventilated that it produces a sickening effect upon him.

Q. Then he does not get upon the level where they are, and pass between the rows of them, helping each one singly?

A. He should do it, but from the excessively filthy state it is not always done.

Q. He has to get upon a mass of filth?

A. He has to get upon a mass of filth, and almost upon a mass of living bodies at the same time, because they roll out and take up every thing they can.

Q. In that case some may go without food?

A. Frequently those that are more remote do not get any thing at all, unless they can crawl up over the others and get nearer to the hatchways.

Q. In the case of one of these people dying, how is the body removed?

A. It lies there until perhaps an alarm is given or something like that, and in the morning it is generally thrown overboard.

Q. Is it always noticed?

A. There may be instances, and I believe there have been instances in which they have remained until they have increased the amount of putridity, and in fact when they have been thrown overboard, you could hardly keep them together; because the putrefaction would be so rapid in a temperature of of that kind, that in a few hours decomposition would take place; they would hardly hold together to be thrown overboard. * * * *

Q. When the cargoes come in, are the slaves, or a great many of them, unable to walk?

A. Most of them are.

Q. Are these men shackled?

A. No, the little ones which they bring now are not shackled. The most favourite cargoes, at the present time, are boys of eight to twelve years of age.

Q. Why do they bring them at so early an age?

A. Because at that age they are smaller and pack more conveniently, and will endure the effects of the voyage better than persons of more mature age. * * * * * * * *

Q. Have you seen many cases of the slaves landed from the slavers on their arrival?

A. Yes.

Q. In what condition did you find them?

A. I do not know that I could describe it, to be intelligible to you. I do not think that I have power of description enough to describe it.

Q. You have told us these three things, that they are, many of them, in a situation of acute suffering, and at the same time of great physical reduction and torpidity of the animal functions.

A. Yes; so that the knee bones appear almost like the head of a person; from the arm you may slip your finger and thumb up; the muscular part of the arm is gone, it is a mere bone covered with a bit of skin; the abdomen is highly protuberant, it is very much distended, very large. I am speaking of them just as they are landed. A man takes them up in his arms and carries them out of the vessel; you have some slave, or some person that must do it if they are not capable of walking; they are pulled out and those that are very dirty are washed. * * *

Q. Are they for the most part lifted up on deck?

A. A great many of them are; a good many make attempts, they could not stand even if they were not so much emaciated. From not having perhaps stood upright for a month or two, the muscles have lost the power of supporting them.

Q. The eye has lost its speculation?

A. Precisely so; it has an idiotic appearance, a leaden appearance, in fact a sunk appearance. It is almost like the boiled eye of a fish. In fact nature is reduced to the very last stage consistent with life. To the lowest stage in which it is possible to say they are yet living. * * *

Q. Have you ever formed an estimate of the numbers who perish after they are landed?

A. No. In some vessels where the captain is a humane and clever man, the mortality is always a great deal less. Where the man is a humane man and has plenty of resources within himself, the amount of positive suffering is never so great; but with those who are more careless the sufferings are indescribable. There is every thing bad that you can either mention or fancy."—*2d Rep. to H. C.*, 1848, *p.* 42–50.

Such is the picture drawn by one who had himself actively participated in the scenes which he describes. The heart instinctively revolts at the dreadful details, and we feel unwilling to believe that any of our kind can become so lost to every human feeling, as voluntarily to engage in a business almost inseparably connected with so much cruelty and degradation. And yet the conviction is forced upon us, that large numbers of our own countrymen are devoting their time, their strength and their wealth to its eager pursuit, and that through them the rights and privileges of American citizenship are degraded into the means for maintaining this system of wholesale murder and indescribable misery.

It is not merely the captains and crews of the American vessels, who are carrying from a foreign port "goods to the coast," and returning crammed with cargoes of human flesh and blood, that are guilty of the multiform crimes of the trade, and should be held responsible therefor; but not a few it is to be feared here in our own country, men who perhaps are occupying respectable stations in society, and are received and associated with as honourable citizens,—high professors it may be of the Christian religion, are acting as agents for supplying these vessels, shipping their crews, and securing to them the protection of the national flag, and are therefore equally criminal and equally deserving of condemnation.

Nor can our National government justly escape a portion of the censure that attaches to all, who either directly or indirectly connive at and facilitate its pursuit, or screen from punishment those who are embarked in it. More than five years have now elapsed since our Minister at Brazil, clearly demonstrated to those in authority at Washington, the manner and the extent in which the African Slave trade is dependent for its successful prosecution, upon the American marine and the use of the American flag, and the attention of the government has since then been called again and again to the subject, in order that it might take some step to put a stop to the crying evil. Nothing however has been done that can avail in counteracting and breaking up the schemes of the Slave dealers.

By treaty stipulations with Great Britain, a naval force is employed on the African coast, but it has been, and can be of very little use as a police, for the prevention of the illicit trade. By government orders, the Consuls have been forbidden to exercise any discretion in granting sea-letters in cases of sale of a vessel by one American citizen to another in a foreign port, and we have seen how completely these credentials are made subservient to the interests of the Slave traders. Under their protection their vessels visit all parts of the African coast, secure from molestation by the American cruizers, and prepared, if visited by the cruizers of other nations, to give colour to the bitter complaints which they do not fail to raise in order to arouse the jealousy with which our government has ever resisted the right of search.

So great is the extent of coast from which slaves can be shipped, and so constantly do the traders change the places of embarkation, that the few vessels employed by the American government are easily deceived and avoided. Even when they do overhaul vessels connected with the trade, so difficult is it in the courts of this country to convict upon the ground of equipment, that the officers knowing they may be made liable for damages should the case not be made out, are unwilling to run the risk, and very often both principal and accomplices are suffered to escape with impunity. Even where the cargo of slaves has been found on board, suffering the horrid tortures of the middle passage, the aggressors have either managed to elude the demands of justice by a sham transfer to another nationality, or in some other way have escaped the punishment they deserved.

In almost every instance, if not in all, where conviction has followed trial in this country, the guilty party has been rescued from the penalty of the law, however richly deserved, by the means of an Executive pardon.

The question naturally arises, how are these evils to be met and overcome. Within the last few years they have been too glaring, and too repeatedly denounced by other governments, to be concealed, or to be passed by in silence by our Executive. The subject has therefore been brought before Congress, by Presidents Tyler, Polk, and Taylor, but without any decisive action being taken. During the last session of Congress it was again brought under discussion, and much was said respecting the enormity of the crime, and the necessity of rescuing the stars and stripes from the odium attached to them by their employment in this disgraceful commerce, but amid the pressure of other business, this could not obtain sufficient time and attention to allow any legislative measures to be perfected, and consequently nothing can be done in that way, until Congress shall meet again.

But it is greatly to be desired that no more time may be lost, and that whatever course may be pursued, it shall be fully adequate to meet the whole case, and to cut the evil up by the root. Both the present Minister at Brazil and his predecessor, have assured our government that there is no commerce between Brazil and Africa, but what is either directly or indirectly connected with and dependent upon the Slave trade, and that our ship owners and merchants may rely on their assertion, if they are not already aware of the fact, that the reason why their vessels yield so large a profit, either when sold in, or sailed under a charter-party from the different ports of Brazil, is because they are to be employed in the African Slave trade.

We have seen by the despatch already given from the present Minister to that country, that he recommends "all trade in vessels of the United States, between the ports of Brazil and those of Africa, to be prohibited by law." "That it be declared criminal to sell any American vessel on the coast of Africa, unless when condemned as unseaworthy, after survey made according to law, and that it be declared criminal to sell, anywhere an American vessel deliverable on the coast of Africa."

We do not know that the enactment of laws for carrying these provisions into effect, would be sufficient, or be the wisest course to pursue for attaining the end proposed, but we think that if they are required therefor, the pecuniary sacrifice, however great it might be, should not be allowed to come in competition with the demands of justice and humanity.

During the period which we have been reviewing, the progress of the cause of human rights among the nations of the earth, has been decided and increasing, and we cannot doubt that as light and knowledge are more generally diffused, as the Spirit of the Gospel is more fully recognised, and its requirements carried into effect by the governments professing to believe in it, this cause must continue to triumph over the obstacles that oppose it until it shall not only have destroyed the trade carried on in the sons and daughters of Africa; but until slavery itself shall have ceased to exist, and their descendants shall have regained all the rights of which they have been deprived, by violence and fraud. We have seen that much has been done in that time, in conformity with the demands of justice and the obligations of the divine law in relation to the suppression of the Slave trade, and the emancipation of the enslaved. The National Assembly of France, while asserting and securing by constitutional provisions the liberty of the citizens of that country, recognized the right of the coloured man to personal freedom as equal to their own, and decreed the abolition of slavery throughout all her colonies, so that a slave cannot exist within the limits of that Republic.* Denmark has shown her wisdom and her sense of justice, by pursuing the same course, for although the first act, providing for the extinction of slavery in her dominions, contemplated its completion within twelve years, yet subsequent events evinced the propriety of immediate emancipation, and the slaves were at once released from their servitude. Sweden, rather than rest under the odium connected with the support of the iniquitous system, voluntarily paid the price of the few hundred slaves held by her subjects, and restored them to freedom. Portugal, who had so long and so perseveringly pursued the trade in men, has not only subjected her subjects convicted of participating therein, to the penalty awarded to piracy, but entertained the project of a law which will probably soon be adopted for abolishing slavery in those parts of her

* By this act between 250,000 and 300,000 slaves were at once declared free.

dominions where it exists. Even some of the powers which we style barbarous, have joined in the general condemnation of the trade, and one of them emancipated upwards of 30,000 slaves at once, declaring what it would be well for us to remember, "that the servitude imposed on a part of the human kind whom God has created, is a very cruel thing."

By means of treaties with native chiefs resident on or near the coast, by the settlement at Sierra Leone, Liberia, and other stations, and by the intervention of an armed police constantly on the watch, to prevent the violation of the laws of the civilized world against the African Slave trade, large districts of country where the manstealer and his accomplices once had unrestricted sway and full license to pursue their iniquitous commerce, have been rescued from their polluting and desolating presence.

But though such is the fact, it is nevertheless evident, that within the last five years the Slave trade has greatly revived and augmented, until it is probable that from 85,000 to 100,000 victims are annually required to satisfy its demands. We have seen that its cruelties and its crimes are in no wise diminished; and as the knowledge of right and wrong is spread abroad, its guilt is proportionally increased.

Spain and Brazil actuated by a blind policy, appear willing to bear the disgrace, and to incur the penalty of being its chief supporters, for the sake of supplying the supposed wants of their people; but our own country is deeply implicated therein, and made to share largely in the odium and guilt, in order that her citizens may earn the gold paid them as common carriers, who, under the protection of her flag, traverse the great highway of nations with their vessels crammed to suffocation with wretched victims. It behooves all to be alive to the enormity of the evil, and to the responsibility resting upon us, both individually and as a nation, and to exert whatever influence we may possess, until our fellow countrymen shall voluntarily desist from all connection with this trade, or until our government shall enact such laws for its suppression, as will effectually prevent them from pursuing it.

FINIS.

www.ingramcontent.com/pod-product-compliance
Lightning Source LLC
LaVergne TN
LVHW021402110826
845150LV00007B/1754

* 9 7 8 1 4 2 5 5 1 2 0 6 4 *